LEARN
RUSSIAN
(RUSKI)
THE FAST AND FUN WAY

Second Edition

by Thomas R. Beyer, Jr., Ph.D.
C.V. Starr Professor of Russian
Middlebury College
Middlebury, Vermont

To help you pace your learning, we've included
stopwatches *like the one above* throughout
the book to mark each 15-minute interval.
You can read one of these units each day
or pace yourself according to your needs.

BARRON'S

CONTENTS

Pronunciation 2
The Russian Alphabet. 6

GETTING TO KNOW PEOPLE. . . 8
1 Let's Get Acquainted 8

ARRIVAL. 21
2 Where to Spend the Night 21

PLACES OF INTEREST 29
3 How to Get There (on Foot) 29
4 Means of Transportation/How to Get
   There (by Vehicle) 35
5 Time and Numbers 41
6 On the Train 54
7 Countries and Languages 60
8 On the Road 68
9 How We Vacation 80
10 Seasons of the Year, Months, Weather,
   Days of the Week 84
11 Airplanes. 91

ENTERTAINMENT 100
12 Theater, Movies, Holidays 100
13 Sport(s) 108

ORDERING A MEAL 112
14 Breakfast, Lunch/Dinner, Supper 112
15 The Restaurant/Tips 120

HOW ARE WE DOING? 124

AT THE STORE 130
16 Clothing, Sizes, Colors 130
17 The Supermarket 136
18 Drugstore/Pharmacy 143
19 Laundry/Dry Cleaner's 149
20 Beauty Salon/Barber Shop 153
21 The Newsstand/Stationery Goods/
   Office Supplies 158
22 Jewelry Articles/Watches 162
23 Gifts, Souvenirs, Music, Cameras . . . 167
24 Repair Services: Eyeglasses, Shoes . . 173

ESSENTIAL SERVICES. 176
25 Bank/Savings Bank 176
26 Mail/Post Office/Internet 182
27 Telephone 188
28 Doctor, Dentist, Hospital 192
29 Help! 201

BEFORE YOU LEAVE 204

VOCABULARY CARDS 213

© Copyright 2009 and 1993 by Barron's Educational Series, Inc.

All rights reserved. No part of this publication may be reproduced or distributed in any form or by any means without the written permission of the copyright owner.

All inquiries should be addressed to:
Barron's Educational Series, Inc.
250 Wireless Boulevard
Hauppauge, NY 11788
www.barronseduc.com

ISBN-13: 978-0-7641-4214-7
ISBN-10: 0-7641-4214-3
Library of Congress Control Number: 2009927791

Printed in China

9 8 7 6 5

For Dorothea, Carina, Stefanie and Alexandra.

With gratitude to all my Russian friends, to countless key ladies, shop clerks, hairdressers, diplomats, scholars, colleagues, and all those lovely people who have made Russian fun for me.

INTRODUCTION TO THE SECOND EDITION AND HINTS ON USING THE BOOK

Some things change, some things stay the same. The Russia of today is in many ways far removed from the country just emerging from the shadows of the Communist state in the early 1990s. Anyone who had experienced the monotonous bleakness of Russian stores and the steady and dependable prices for public transportation, just five kopecks for the metro, would be dazed by the glamour, street lights, and choices that Russians have available to them today. Political freedom, a free press, consumerism, the ability to travel freely, Russians now enjoy the same privileges and responsibilities as their European neighbors.

The world too has changed. When I was writing the first edition of this book the World Wide Web was just beginning. Cell phones were bulky, expensive, and in the hands of few. Personal computing was gaining popularity, but its uses were limited. The Internet was not widely accessible, and a few e-mails a week seemed quite a lot. The digital age as we know it in the twenty-first century had just begun to emerge. So there is much that is new in Russia and in the Russian language.

Yet the basic grammatical structure and vocabulary remain the same. The rules for the formation of the plural or for conjugating verbs are the same now as they were fifteen years ago.

My goal was then and is today to provide you with a book that helps you learn some basics of Russian and permit you to have some fun along the way. A few hints as you start out. Learning the letters of the alphabet and how to pronounce Russian words is easy to master. We have often given you a transcription, an approximation of how a Russian word is pronounced, in *italics*. These can be useful especially at the start, but remember that Russians transliterate in only a few instances, such as international road signs. So you would be wise to learn the alphabet as soon as possible. At the back of the book you will find a *Russian–English English–Russian Dictionary*. The English to Russian section gives the transcription as a pronunciation guide for every Russian word in our book. If you are ever in doubt you can look back to refresh your memory. Take this book a little at a time. It is better to read, pronounce aloud and write a section several times and really master it, than to try rushing through the materials. In language, tiny differences in spelling and pronunciation can make huge distinctions in meaning. It is better to be precise. As you work your way through the book, try to use all your senses. Look at a word, say it aloud and listen to it, write it out in cursive. Russian and English speakers alike know the Latin proverb "Repetition is the mother of learning." So practice often.

We have used the colors blue, pink, and yellow, to point out key words and concepts. Be sure that you know and understand them and can remember them without the aid of the book.

Finally, if you have comments or suggestions, send me an e-mail at tom.beyer@middlebury.edu

The Author

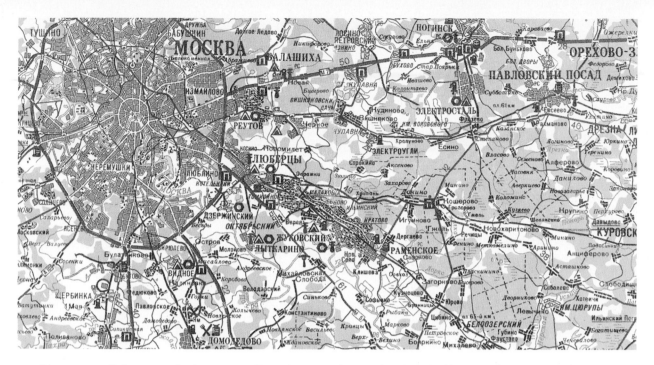

For most of the twentieth century Russia was the largest and most influential of the fifteen republics that made up the Union of Soviet Socialist Republics (USSR) or the Soviet Union. Even after its breakup in 1991, Russia has emerged as still the largest country in the world, occupying almost one-sixth of our planet's land mass, and Russian influence and Russian people still exert a significant presence in many of the former republics. The vast expanses of the country cover eleven separate time zones on two continents: Europe and Asia. Russia has approximately 140 million people, almost half of the inhabitants of the former Soviet Union. All are citizens of Russia (**россияне**), and many are ethnic Russians (**русские**). Russia, however, is a multinational state and home to over one hundred nationalities and languages.

The Russian language was a mandatory subject in Soviet schools and almost all of the 265 million people inhabiting the former republics know and speak Russian, either as their native or second language. In fact, a Georgian who wishes to speak with an Uzbek is likely to use Russian for communication. While English and other languages are now gaining popularity, Russian will likely continue to be understood for at least another generation in all of the former republics: Armenia, Azerbaijan, Belarus, Estonia, Georgia, Latvia, Lithuania, Kazakhstan, Kyrgyzstan, Moldova, Russia, Tajikistan, Turkmenistan, Ukraine, Uzbekistan.

Knowing Russian can open up a window onto a fascinating and enchanting nation, from the fairytale cupolas of Saint Basil's Cathedral to the majesty and power of Red Square and the Kremlin. Moscow, Russia's capital, is home to more than ten million people and the world-renowned Bolshoi Ballet. Far to the north, Saint Petersburg, capital to the tsars from Peter the Great until Nicholas II, offers a marvelous blend of picturesque architecture highlighted by the White Nights of summer. Here too are the glorious palaces—the magnificent Winter Palace and Hermitage Art Museum.

Russians take great pride in their culture and country and they appreciate the efforts of those who try to speak their language. For many, the Russian alphabet is a major stumbling block to getting to know the country and its people better. With our *Fast and Fun Way* you'll be reading the signs and ready to talk with real Russians in just a matter of days. When you do get an opportunity to use your new language skills, you'll notice that your efforts will be truly rewarded. So let's begin!

1

PRONUNCIATION

You know you're in Russia when the simple sign for a restaurant looks like **РЕСТОРАН.** Actually, the Russian alphabet has only a few more letters than English. But to get started, look at the list below. Read aloud the pronunciation in the first column and then look at the Russian letters in the middle column. At the far right you will see the translation, and you'll be pleasantly surprised to learn how many of them you already know. After the first three words we'll add only one new letter per word.

Pronunciation	Russian	English
DA	ДА	yes
NYET	НЕТ	no
BANK	БАНК	bank
BAR	БАР	bar
PARK	ПАРК	park
KAsa	КАССА	cashier
taKSI	ТАКСИ	taxi
kiOSK	КИОСК	kiosk, newsstand
kaFE	КАФЕ	café
buFYET	БУФЕТ	buffet, snack bar
miTRO	МЕТРО	metro, subway
maskVA	МОСКВА	Moscow
aeraPORT	АЭРОПОРТ	airport
aeraFLOT	АЭРОФЛОТ	Aeroflot
ZAL	ЗАЛ	hall
FKHOT	ВХОД	entrance
VYkhat	ВЫХОД	exit
TSENTR	ЦЕНТР	center
byuRO	БЮРО	bureau
gardiROP	ГАРДЕРОБ	garderobe, coat check
POCHta	ПОЧТА	post office
RYAT	РЯД	row
STOYtye	СТОЙТЕ	Stand!
nye kuRIT'	НЕ КУРИТЬ	No Smoking
bal'SHOY	БОЛЬШОЙ	the Bolshoi, big
ZHENski	ЖЕНСКИЙ	ladies' (room)
muSHKOY	МУЖСКОЙ	men's (room)
yiSCHO	ЕЩЁ	more, else

2

Now that you have seen most of the Russian letters, let's look at the whole system. What we commonly call the Russian alphabet is officially known as the Cyrillic alphabet. The Russians adopted the Cyrillic alphabet created in the ninth century when the monks Cyril and Methodius developed a written language for the Slavs. The Cyrillic alphabet has thirty-three letters and has much in common with the Greek alphabet. As you have seen, many letters are familiar to you from English and several others resemble Greek letters. As in English, each letter is only an approximation of how a sound is pronounced. The guide below should get you started in speaking Russian.

VOWELS

Russian has five vowel sounds, but ten vowel letters. Five of the letters are "hard" and five are "soft." The one vowel sound in each word that is stressed receives special emphasis. As you speak Russian, try in the beginning to exaggerate your pronunciation.

Russian Letter	Russian Sound	English Symbol	Example	
Hard Vowels				
а	**a** as in f**a**ther	A	да	*DA*
э	**e** as in **e**cho	E	эхо	*Ekho*
ы	**y** as in hair**y**	Y	мы	*MY*
о	**o** as in hell**o**	O	но	*NO*
у	**u** as in r**u**le	U	ну	*NU*
Soft Vowels				
я	**ya** as in **ya**hoo	YA	я	*YA*
е	**ye** as in **ye**s	YE	нет	*NYET*
и	**ee** as in b**ee**	I	ива	*Iva*
ё	**yo** as in **yo**-yo	YO	полёт	*paLYOT*
ю	**u** as in **u**nion	YU	юмор	*YUmar*

CONSONANT LETTERS

Russian Letter	Russian Sound	English Symbol	Example
б	**b** as in **b**at	B	банк *BANK*
в	**v** as in **v**ote	V	вот *VOT*
г	**g** as in **g**o	G	гол *GOL*
д	**d** as in **d**og	D	да *DA*
ж	**zh** as in a**z**ure	ZH	жена *zhiNA*
з	**z** as in **z**oo	Z	за *ZA*
й	**y** as in bo**y**	Y	мой *MOY*
к	**k** as in **k**ayak	K	касса *KAsa*
л	**l** as in **l**ot	L	лампа *LAMpa*
м	**m** as in **m**all	M	муж *MUSH*
н	**n** as in **n**ote	N	нос *NOS*
п	**p** as in **p**apa	P	парк *PARK*
р	**r** as in **r**abbit	R	рот *ROT*
с	**s** as in **s**un	S	суп *SUP*
т	**t** as in **t**oe	T	такси *taKSI*
ф	**f** as in **f**und	F	фунт *FUNT*
х	**ch** as in Ba**ch**, lo**ch**	KH	ах *AKH*
ц	**ts** as in **ts**ar	TS	царь *TSAR'*
ч	**ch** as in **ch**eap	CH	читает *chiTAyit*
ш	**sh** as in **sh**ow	SH	шапка *SHAPka*
щ	**sh** as in **sh**eep	SCH	щи *SCHI*
ъ	hard sign		not pronounced
ь	soft sign		not pronounced

Each Russian word has only one syllable that is stressed or under accent. Russians simply know where the stress is and do not write the accent marks. We will indicate the stressed syllable in our transcription with capital letters as an aid for your pronunciation.

The Russian letter **ё** is rarely written with two dots over it. Russians simply know the correct pronunciation. In dictionaries words beginning with the letter **ё** are listed under the letter **e**.

THREE RULES OF PRONUNCIATION

1. Russians pronounce the **o** sound only when it is stressed. When some other vowel is stressed in a word, the letter **o** is pronounced as an **a**—кот (*KOT*), but котá (*kaTA*). When the letters **е, я** and sometimes **a** are not stressed, they are pronounced as **i** in the English word "it."

2. Consonants can be hard **ну** (*NU*) or soft **нет** (*NYET*). The soft **n** is like the sound in the word "onion." A consonant is hard unless it is followed by a soft vowel letter **я, е, и, ё, ю** or by the soft sign **ь**.

3. At the end of a word, or before voiced consonants, **б, в, г, д, ж,** and **з,** become their voiceless counterparts, **б→п, в→ф, г→к, д→т, ж→ш, з→с.** Examples: **год**→*GOT,* **баб**→*BAP,* **ног**→ *NOK,* **автомат**→*aftaMAT,* **водка**→*VOTka.*

Now look at the following Russian signs and see if you can write their meanings in the blanks.

1. **СУВЕНИРЫ** _____

2. **ТЕЛЕФОН** _____

3. **РЕСТОРАН** _____

4. **ТУАЛЕТ** _____

5. **ТЕАТР** _____

ANSWERS

1. SOUVENIRS 2. TELEPHONE 3. RESTAURANT 4. RESTROOM (TOILET/WC) 5. THEATER

THE RUSSIAN ALPHABET

Now that we know how to pronounce Russian letters and words, it's time to learn how to recognize the letters of the alphabet and to write them. As in English, Russian has printed or **block** letters and cursive or *italic* letters. One major difference, however, is that Russians do not print. So while you want to be able to recognize both sets of letters, you'll want to use the cursive letters when you write. Below is the Russian alphabet in its alphabetical order. Next to it we have given the English. Finally, there are spaces for you to try your hand at writing Russian.

Russian		English		Your turn
А а	*Аа*	A a	*Аа*	_____
Б б	*Бб*	B b	*Вb*	_____
В в	*Вв*	V v	*Vv*	_____
Г г	*Гг*	G g	*Gg*	_____
Д д	*Дд*	D d	*Dd*	_____
Е е	*Ее*	Ye ye	*Ye ye*	_____
Ё ё	*Ёё*	Yo yo	*Yo yo*	_____
Ж ж	*Жж*	Zh zh	*Zh zh*	_____
З з	*Зз*	Z z	*Z z*	_____
И и	*Ии*	I i	*Ii*	_____
Й й	*Йй*	Y y	*Yy*	_____
К к	*Кк*	K k	*Kk*	_____
Л л	*Лл*	L l	*Ll*	_____

Мм	*Мм*	M m	*Mm*	_____
Нн	*Нн*	N n	*Nn*	_____
Оо	*Оо*	O o	*Oo*	_____
Пп	*Пп*	P p	*Pp*	_____
Рр	*Рр*	R r	*Rr*	_____
Сс	*Сс*	S s	*Ss*	_____
Тт	*Тт*	T t	*Tt*	_____
Уу	*Уу*	U u	*Uu*	_____
Фф	*Фф*	F f	*Ff*	_____
Хх	*Хх*	Kh kh	*Kh kh*	_____
Цц	*Цц*	Ts ts	*Ts ts*	_____
Чч	*Чч*	Ch ch	*Ch ch*	_____
Шш	*Шш*	Sh sh	*Sh sh*	_____
Щщ	*Щщ*	Sch sch	*Sch sch*	_____
ъ	*ъ*			_____
ы	*ы*	y	*y*	_____
ь	*ь*			_____
Ээ	*Ээ*	E e	*Ee*	_____
Юю	*Юю*	Yu yu	*Yu yu*	_____
Яя	*Яя*	Ya ya	*Ya ya*	_____

GETTING TO KNOW PEOPLE
(znaKOMSTva)
Знакомство

1	*(daVAYtye)* *(paznaKOmimsya)* ## Давайте познакомимся. Let's Get Acquainted.	

Knowing how to greet people and start a conversation is very important. Read the following dialogue several times, pronouncing each line carefully aloud. The dialogue contains basic words and expressions that will be useful to you.

Mark Smith, his wife, Caroline, their daughter, Stephanie, and their son, Alex, have just arrived at **Шереметьево** (Sheremetevo) airport in **Москва** (Moscow) and are looking for their luggage. Mark approaches an airline employee.

MARK	*(ZDRASTvuytye)* **Здравствуйте.**	Hello.
CLERK	**Здравствуйте.**	Hello.
	(paMOCH) **Как вам помочь?**	How may I help you?
MARK	*(GDYE) (NAshi) (chimaDAny)* **Где наши чемоданы?**	Where are our suitcases?
CLERK	*(zaVUT)* **Как вас зовут?**	What is your name?
MARK	*(miNYA)* **Меня зовут "Mark Smith."**	My name is Mark Smith.

8

CLERK	*(atKUda)* **Откуда вы?**	Where are you from?
MARK	*(YA) (IS) (SA SHA A)* **Я из США.**	I'm from the USA.
CLERK	*(NOmir) (VAshiva) (RYEYsa)* **Номер вашего рейса?**	Your flight number?
MARK	**Аэрофлот 62.**	Aeroflot 62.

As the clerk looks through some papers on her desk, **Иван** (Ivan), Mark's host in Moscow, approaches.

ИВАН	*(priVYET)* *(diLA)* **Привет, Марк. Как дела?**	Hi, Mark. How are things?
MARK	*(kharaSHO) (spaSIba)* **Хорошо, спасибо.**	Fine, thanks.
ИВАН	*(BYL)* *(paLYOT)* **Как был ваш полет?**	How was your flight?
MARK	*(maYA) (siMYA)* **Вот моя семья,** *(zhiNA)* **моя жена.**	Here is my family, my wife
ИВАН	*(Ochin') (priYATna)* **Очень приятно.**	A pleasure to meet you.
MARK	*(DOCHka)* **И это дочка** *(SYN)* **и сын.**	And here are my daughter and son.
CLERK	*(izviNItye)* *(paZHAlusta)* **Извините, пожалуйста.** **Ваши чемоданы** *(aSTAlis')* **остались в Вашингтоне.**	Excuse me, please. Your suitcases stayed behind in Washington.
MARK	*(tiPYER')* *(DYElat')* **А теперь что нам делать?**	And now what are we to do?
CLERK	*(valNUYtyes')* **Не волнуйтесь.** *(aNI) (BUdut)* **Они будут в Москве** *(ZAFtra)* **завтра.**	Don't worry. They'll be in Moscow tomorrow.
MARK	*(LUche)* *(POZna)* *(CHEM)* *(nikagDA)* **Лучше поздно, чем никогда.**	Better late than never.
CLERK	*(PRAvy)* **Вы правы.**	You are right.
ИВАН	*(paSHLI)* **Ну пошли.**	Well, let's get going.

	(da) (sviDAniya)	
MARK	До свидания.	Goodbye.
CLERK	До свидания.	Goodbye.

Now here is your first exercise based on the dialogue you have practiced. Try to match the Russian expressions from the dialogue with their English equivalents. No peeking until you've tried.

1. **Хорошо, спасибо.**

2. **Здравствуйте.**

3. **Как вам помочь?**

4. **До свидания.**

5. **Не волнуйтесь.**

6. **Как вас зовут?**

7. **Ну, пошли.**

8. **Лучше поздно, чем никогда.**

9. **Извините, пожалуйста.**

10. **Очень приятно.**

a. Don't worry.

b. What's your name?

c. Better late than never.

d. Fine, thanks.

e. Excuse me, please.

f. How may I help you?

g. Goodbye.

h. Hello.

i. A pleasure (to meet you).

j. Well, let's get going.

(LYUdi) *(i)* *(VYEschi)*

ЛЮДИ И ВЕЩИ

People and things

One of the first things you'll have to know in Russian is how to name people and things. These are the *nouns*, the naming words. Russian nouns belong to one of three grammatical genders. They can be masculine, feminine, or neuter, and you can usually tell the gender of a noun by the ending. Masculine nouns end in a consonant. Feminine nouns end in **а** or **я**. Neuter nouns end in **о** or **е**. Some nouns end in the soft sign **ь**; most of these are feminine except for ones ending in **-ель**, which are masculine. The gender is only a grammatical category. The Russian

(STUL) *(riKA)* *(pis'MO)*
word for chair, **стул**, is masculine. River, **река**, is feminine. A letter, **письмо**, is neuter.

English forms the plural by adding the letter **s (es)** to the end of a word. Russian plurals can be formed by ending **ы (и)** or **а (я)**.

(stuDYENT) *(stuDYENty)*
If the noun ends in a consonant, add **ы** to the ending, **студент→студенты**.

(KOMnata) *(KOMnaty)*
If the noun ends in **а**, replace the **а** with **ы**, **комната→комнаты**.

(TYOtya) (TYOti)
If the noun ends in the soft sign **ь** or the letter **я**, add **и**, **тётя→тёти**.

(pis'MO) *(PIS'ma)*
For neuter nouns that end in **о**, change the **о** to **а**, **письмо→письма**.

(ZDAniye) *(ZDAniya)*
If the ending was **е** change that **е** to **я**, **здание→здания**.

SPELLING RULES

There are a few spelling rules you should learn to help you with the formation of endings. The main principle is that hard endings tend to stay hard, and soft endings tend to stay soft. We say an ending is hard if it ends in a hard sign **ъ**, or a consonant except **й**, or is followed by one of the so-called hard vowels: **а, э, ы, о, у**.

An ending is soft if it ends in a soft sign **ь**, or is followed by one of the soft vowels: **я, е, и, ё, ю**.

Another useful rule is that after the letters **г, к, х, ч, ш, щ, ж**, you may not write the letter **ы**. Instead, you must write an **и**.

(MAL'chik) *(MAL'chiki),* *(stuDYENTka)* *(stuDYENTki)*
EXAMPLE: **мальчик→мальчики, студентка→студентки**

Singular and Plural

(yiDINSTvinaye)   *(chiSLO)*
единственное число
singular   number

(MNOzhistvinaye)   *(chiSLO)*
множественное число
plural   number

(STOL)
стол
table

(staLY)
столы
tables

(afTObus)
автобус
bus

(afTObusy)
автобусы
buses

(LAMpa)
лампа
lamp

(LAMpy)
лампы
lamps

(gaZYEta)
газета
newspaper

(gaZYEty)
газеты
newspapers

(MAL'chik)
мальчик
boy

(MAL'chiki)
мальчики
boys

единственное число	**множественное число**

(DYEvushka)
девушка
girl

(DYEvushki)
девушки
girls

_____

_____

(naGA)
нога
leg

(NOgi)
ноги
legs

_____

_____

(pis'MO)
письмо
letter

(PIS'ma)
письма
letters

_____

_____

(okNO)
окно
window

(OKna)
окна
windows

_____

_____

(ZDAniye)
здание
building

(ZDAniya)
здания
buildings

_____

_____

Before going on, review the above words and write them out in the blanks provided.

Just as English has its "child" but "children," "woman" but "women," Russian has some plurals that simply should be learned. Here are a few of the most important ones. Repeat them to yourself and then write them out.

13

(MAT')
мать
mother

(MAtiri)
матери
mothers

(aTYETS)
отец
father

(aTSY)
отцы
fathers

(DOCH)
дочь
daughter

(DOchiri)
дочери
daughters

(SYN)
сын
son

(synaV'YA)
сыновья
sons

(riBYOnak)
ребёнок
child

(DYEti)
дети
children

Now, give the name of the famous Russian novel *Fathers and Sons*.

(Hint: It was actually *Fathers and Children*.) _____

ANSWER

Novel Отцы и дети

14

(ON) *(aNA)* *(aNO)*
ОН, ОНА, ОНО
Не/it   she/it   it

We now know that Russian nouns are identified by their grammatical gender. Examine the following questions and answers.

(GDYE) *(afTObus)* **Где автобус?** Where's the bus?	*(ON)* *(TAM)* **Он там.** It's over there.
(GDYE) *(STANtsiya)* *(miTRO)* **Где станция метро?** Where's the Metro station?	*(aNA)* *(TAM)* **Она там.** It's over there.
(GDYE) *(pis'MO)* **Где письмо?** Where's the letter?	*(aNO)* *(TAM)* **Оно там.** It's over there.

(aNI)

In the plural, all of the genders are replaced by only one form of the pronoun: **они**.

(GDYE) *(gaZYEty)* **Где газеты?** Where are the newspapers?	*(aNI)* *(TAM)* **Они там.** They're over there.

Now try to fill in the blanks with the correct form of **он, она, оно, они**.

(GDYE) *(stuDYENT)*
1. Где студент?
Where's the student?

(TAM)
_____ **там.**
there.

(GDYE) *(DYEriva)*
2. Где дерево?
Where's the tree?

(TAM)
_____ **там.**
there.

(GDYE) *(KNIga)*
3. Где книга?
Where's the book?

(TAM)
_____ **там.**
there.

15

(GDYE) (YABlaka)

4. Где яблоко?

Where's the apple?

_____ **там.**

there.

(GDYE) (DYEti)

5. Где дети?

Where are the children?

_____ **там.**

there.

(GDYE) (MAma)

6. Где мама?

Where's Mama?

_____ **там.**

there.

(GDYE) (DOM)

7. Где дом?

Where's the house?

_____ **там.**

there.

(GDYE) (maskVA)

8. Где Москва?

Where's Moscow?

_____ **там.**

there.

Let's see how many Russian words you can write in the blanks below. Notice how Russians can ask questions with the following little words: **кто** (who), **что** (what), **где** (where).

(KTO)   (Eta)

1. Кто это?

Who is that?

(Eta)

Это _____.

That's a student.

(SHTO)

2. Что это?

What is that?

Это _____.

That's a book.

16

3. *(GDYE)*
Где _____ **?**

Where is the house?

(VOT)
Вот он.

Here it is!

4. Где _____ **?**
Where is Moscow?

Вот она.

Here it is!

5. Где _____ **?**

Where is the apple?

Вот оно.

Here it is!

6. Где _____ **?**

Where are the children?

Вот они.

Here they are!

7. Где _____ **?**

Where is the tree?

Вот оно.

Here it is!

(YA)	*(TY)*	*(ON)*	*(aNA)*	*(aNO)*	*(MY)*	*(VY)*	*(aNI)*

Я, ты, он, она, оно, мы, вы, они
I   you   he/it   she/it   it   we   you   they

We use personal pronouns to relate to one another. Thus, they are essential if you are to understand and speak Russian. Keep your ears attuned for the word **вы**, the polite form of addressing "you." You'll answer with the form **я**, "I," which is in fact the last letter of the Russian alphabet; it is only capitalized if it begins a sentence. The **ты**, "you," form is used between family members and friends, to animals, and between young people of similar ages. When in doubt, you'll be better off using **вы** so as not to offend anyone.

ANSWERS

Fill in 3. дом **4.** Москва **5.** яблоко **6.** дети **7.** дерево

НАШИ РОДСТВЕННИКИ

(NAshi) *(ROTSTviniki)*

Our relatives

This is **Иван**'s family tree. Note the word for each of his relatives.

(maRIya) *(anDRYEyevna)*
Мария Андреевна
(BAbushka)
бабушка
grandmother

(sirGYEY) *(alikSANdravich)*
Сергей Александрович
(DYEdushka)
дедушка
grandfather

(mikhaIL) *(sirGYEyevich)*
Михаил Сергеевич
(aTYETS)
отец
father

(Ana) *(piTROVna)*
Анна Петровна
(MAT')
мать
mother

(baRIS) *(piTROvich)*
Борис Петрович
(DYAdya)
дядя
uncle

(VYEra) *(sirGYEyevna)*
Вера Сергеевна
(TYOtya)
тётя
aunt

(NIna) *(miKHAYlavna)*
Нина Михайловна
(DOCH)
дочь
daughter

(vaSIli) *(miKHAYlavich)*
Василий Михайлович
(SYN)
сын
son

(iRIna) *(baRIsavna)*
Ирина Борисовна
(dvaYUradnaya)
двоюродная сестра
female cousin

(PYOTR) *(baRIsavich)*
Пётр Борисович
(dvaYUradny)
двоюродный брат
male cousin

(siSTRA)
сестра
sister

(BRAT)
брат
brother

(iVAN) *(miKHAYlavich)*
Иван Михайлович

Find the following family members in the family tree and write in the relationship in the blank space.

1. Нина — _____ Василия.
   sister of

2. Борис Петрович — _____ Нины.
   uncle of

3. Мария Андреевна — _____ Михаила Сергеевича.
   mother of

4. Василий Михайлович — _____ Анны Петровны.
   son of

5. Сергей Александрович — _____ Нины.
   grandfather of

In the word search puzzle we have placed the words for "father," "aunt," "uncle," "grandfather," and "sister." See how many you can find.

я	о	е	ь	т	н	т	а	й	к	л	ж
д	т	ё	т	я	т	ё	д	я	д	я	с
х	е	ф	с	д	е	д	у	ш	к	а	л
м	ц	ч	ф	з	т	с	е	с	т	р	а
н	ж	я	ь	щ	я	ш	р	г	ф	с	х

Each family is unique. Use the spaces below to write out some of the Russian words you will need to describe your own family situation.

_____   _____

_____   _____

_____   _____

_____   _____

Отчим (stepfather), **мачеха** (stepmother), **пасынок** (stepson), **падчерица** (stepdaughter), **сводная сестра** (stepsister), **сводный брат** (stepbrother)

ANSWERS

Family 1. сестра 2. дядя 3. мать 4. сын 5. дедушка
Word search отец, тётя, дядя, дедушка, сестра

19

Look at the Russian words below for an apartment. Repeat each of the words several times and then practice writing them in the spaces below.

(kvarTIRA)
КВАРТИРА
An apartment

(KUKHnya)
кухня
kitchen

(DVYER')
дверь
door

(VAnaya)
ванная
bathroom

(khalaDIL'nik)
холодильник
refrigerator

(VAna)
ванна
bathtub

(duKHOFka)
духовка
oven

(RAkavina)
раковина
sink

(gaSTInaya)
гостиная
living room

(SPAL'nya)
спальня
bedroom

(diVAN)
диван
sofa

(SHKAF)
шкаф
closet

(STOL)
стол
table

(STUL)
стул
chair

(kariDOR)
коридор
hallway

(akNO)
окно
window

(kraVAT')
кровать
bed

_____   _____

_____   _____

_____   _____

_____   _____

_____   _____

_____   _____

_____   _____

ARRIVAL

(priYEST)

Приезд

<table>
<tr>
<td>**2**</td>
<td>*(GDYE)*   *(nachiVAT')*
Где ночевать?
Where to Spend the Night</td>
<td></td>
</tr>
</table>

You'll probably already have booked a room either in a hotel or in a private apartment — at least for your first few days in Russia. In fact, unless you have been invited by someone who will arrange for your accommodations, you should not leave home without a reservation. Even so, you'll want to know some basic words and phrases that describe the services and facilities you can expect to find. Learn these words first, and notice how they are used in the dialogues you will read later.

(gaSTInitsa)

гостиница

hotel

(NOmir)

номер

hotel room

(STOimast')

стоимость

cost

(VAnaya)

ванная

bathroom

(DUSH)

душ

shower

(zabraNIravat')

забронировать

to reserve

(diZHURnaya)

дежурная

key lady (floor clerk)

(adminiSTRAtar)

администратор

administrator

(GORnichnaya)

горничная

maid

паспорт

passport

(KLYUCH)

ключ

key

(LIFT)

лифт

elevator

(SKOL'ka)

Сколько?

How much/many?

The numbers are absolutely essential if you wish to get by in Russian. Take a look and try to pronounce the following numbers from one to ten. Then practice your writing in the spaces supplied.

Number	Russian		Pronunciation
0	нуль	_____	*NUL'*
1	один	_____	*aDIN*
2	два	_____	*DVA*
3	три	_____	*TRI*
4	четыре	_____	*chiTYrye*
5	пять	_____	*PYAT'*
6	шесть	_____	*SHEST'*
7	семь	_____	*SYEM'*
8	восемь	_____	*VOsim'*
9	девять	_____	*DYEvit'*
10	десять	_____	*DYEsit'*

Let's see if you can fill in the blanks after the numerals with their correct names. Solve the problems along the way. Note: Plus is **плюс**, Minus is **минус**, Equals is **будет**.

a. 2 _____ + (плюс *PLYUS*) 3 _____ = **будет** *BUdit* _____

б. 5 _____ + (плюс) 2 _____ = **будет** _____

в. 6 _____ + (плюс) 4 _____ = **будет** _____

г. 8 _____ – (минус *MInus*) 7 _____ = **будет** _____

д. 9 _____ – (минус) 6 _____ = **будет** _____

(NOmir) *(v)* *(gaSTInitse)*

номер в гостинице

A room in the hotel

(SHKAF) **шкаф** — chest of drawers

(ZYERkala) **зеркало** — mirror

(LAMpa) **лампа** — lamp

(RAkavina) **раковина** — sink

(palaTYENtse) **полотенце** — towel

(kraVAT') **кровать** — bed

(DUSH) **душ** — shower

(paDUSHka) **подушка** — pillow

(VAna) **ванна** — bathtub

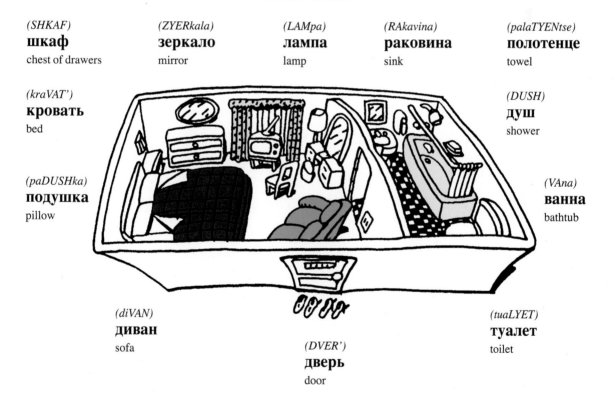

(diVAN) **диван** — sofa

(DVER') **дверь** — door

(tuaLYET) **туалет** — toilet

Как задавать вопрос

How to ask a question

Just like English, Russian has a few essential question words. If most of ours begin with **wh**o, **wh**en, **wh**ere, **wh**at, the Russian question words have **к**то, **к**огда, **к**уда and words derived from those forms, like **г**де and **ч**то.

Look at the words below and repeat them aloud several times. When you feel comfortable that you know them, try writing them out.

Russian word	Pronunciation	English
Кто	*KTO*	Who
Когда	*kagDA*	When
Куда	*kuDA*	Where to
Где	*GDYE*	Where
Что	*SHTO*	What
Как	*KAK*	How
Сколько	*SKOL'ka*	How much, how many

_____   _____   _____   _____

_____   _____   _____

We hope that everything will be perfect, but if something is out of order you may need the following phrases.

(SHTO) (Eta)   *(NYE) (raBOtait)*

Что это? _____ **не работает.**

What is this?   _____   doesn't work.

Can you get the following items repaired?

1. **Что это?**   **Это лампа.**      _____   **не работает.**

ANSWER

2. Что это? Это телевизор. _____ не работает.

3. Что это? Это душ.  _____ не работает.

Let's watch the Smith family check into their hotel. Look at the words carefully and then try to read them aloud to practice your pronunciation.

MARK	Здравствуйте.	Hello.
	(zabraNIravali) **Мы забронировали два**	We reserved two
	(NOmira) *(siVOdnya)* **номера на сегодня.**	rooms for today.
CLERK	*(DObraye)* *(Utra)* **Доброе утро.**	Good morning.
	(faMIliya) **Как ваша фамилия?**	What's your last name?
MARK	**Меня зовут Марк Смит.**	My name is Mark Smith.
CLERK	*(gaspaDIN)* **Да, господин Смит.**	Yes, Mister Smith.
	(DUshem) **Два номера с душем.**	Two rooms with a shower.
	(sazhaLYEniyu) *(adNOM)* **К сожалению, в одном**	Unfortunately, in one
	номере душ не работает.	room the shower isn't working.
MARK	*(nichiVO)* **Ничего. Мы все будем**	It doesn't matter. We'll all
	(priniMAT') *(druGOM)* **принимать душ в другом номере.**	take a shower in the other room.
CLERK	**Хорошо. Но есть ещё**	Fine. But there is still
	(MAlinikaya) *(praBLYEma)* **одна маленькая проблема.**	one small problem.
MARK	*(Imina)* **Что именно?**	What exactly?

CLERK	В другом номере *(akNO) (atkryVAitsa)* окно не открывается.	In the other room the window doesn't open.
MARK (to Caroline)	*(DYElat')* Что будем делать? *(DYEti) (uSTAli)* Поздно. Дети устали. *(svaBODnykh)* Нет свободных номеров во всей Москве.	What shall we do? It's late. The children are tired. There are no available rooms in all of Moscow.
CAROLINE	*(daVAYtye) (aSTAnimsya) (ZDYES')* Давайте останемся здесь.	Let's stay here.
CLERK	Хорошо. *(pasparTA)* Ваши паспорта, *(paZHAluysta)* пожалуйста.	Fine. Your passports, please.
MARK	Вот они. *(naSCHOT)* А как насчёт *(ZAFtraka)* завтрака?	Here they are. And how about breakfast?
CLERK	*(buFYEtye)* Завтрак в буфете *(chiSOF)* в восемь часов. *(prapuSKA)* Вот ваши карты.	Breakfast is served in the snack bar at 8:00 AM. Here are your key cards.*
MARK	*(KLYUCH)* А где номер?	And where is the room?
CLERK	*(shiSTOM) (etaZHE)* На шестом этаже. Номер 615.	On the sixth floor. Room 615.
CAROLINE	*(SKAzhitye)* Вы не скажете, *(LIFT)* где лифт?	Could you tell me where the elevator is?
CLERK	*(iDItye) (PRYAma)* Идите прямо, *(paTOM) (naPRAva)* а потом направо.	Go straight ahead, and then to the right.
MARK	*(spaSIba) (bal'SHOye)* Спасибо большое.	Thank you very much.
CLERK	Пожалуйста.	You're welcome.

*In most hotels you will receive a **Карта гостя** (hotel guest card). This may also serve as your electronic room key. Otherwise you can use the card to obtain your key at the reception desk. Such a key should also be left at the desk whenever you leave the hotel.

After you have reviewed the dialogue a few times, see if you can fill in the blanks with the correct Russian words.

1. Ваши _____ , пожалуйста.

2. Но есть еще одна маленькая _____ .

3. _____ не открывается.

4. А как _____ завтрака?

5. Давайте _____ здесь.

(DVA)   *(SLOva)*

Два слова

Two words

If you want to make friends and get along with people on your trip, you will want to learn and use these two little words.

(spaSIba)	*(paZHAluysta)*
спасибо	**пожалуйста***
thank you	please, you're welcome

*This word can mean either "please" or "you're welcome," according to the situation.

Circle the Russian words for *please* and *thank you* and find another five words related to your hotel stay in the word maze below. (HINT: Look for the Russian words for *elevator, passport, key, maid, toilet.*)

а	б	в	д	к	т	к	л	и	м
п	о	ж	а	л	у	й	с	т	а
а	р	с	у	ю	а	ш	щ	о	ю
с	о	н	т	ч	л	я	б	т	я
п	г	ж	е	э	е	а	с	т	и
о	о	ж	а	л	т	л	и	ф	т
р	й	с	п	а	с	и	б	о	а
т	ё	р	ъ	е	д	м	о	м	ю
г	о	р	н	и	ч	н	а	я	ь

PLACES OF INTEREST

(dastaprimiCHAtil'nasti)
Достопримечательности

3

(KAK)   *(tuDA)*   *(prayTI)*
Как туда пройти?
How to Get There (on Foot)

"How do I get to. . . ?" "Where is the nearest subway?" "Is the museum straight ahead?" You'll be asking directions and getting answers wherever you travel. Get to know the words and phrases that will make getting around easier. Write in the new words and say them aloud several times.

(Ulitsa)
УЛИЦА
Street

(PRYAma)
прямо
straight

Caroline and Mark have just left their hotel for their first morning of sightseeing.

Although they have a map of the city

(PLAN) *(GOrada)*

(**план города**), they decide to try out their new Russian skills and ask the policeman on the corner for directions.

(PLOschat')
площадь
city square

(naLYEva)
налево
to the left

MARK   (to policeman)
Извините. Где

(muZYEY) *(rivaLYUtsiya)*
Музей Революции?
Excuse me. Where is the Museum of the Revolution?

(POCHta)
почта
post office

(naPRAva)
направо
to the right

МИЛИЦИОНЕР   (Policeman)
(iDItye) *(pa)* *(Etay)* *(Ulitse)*
Идите по этой улице
Go along this street

(piriKRYOStak)
перекрёсток
intersection

(svitaFOR)
светофор
traffic light

_____

(da) (svitaFOra)   (paTOM)   (naLYEva)
до светофора, потом налево
until the traffic signal, then to the left

(da)(uGLA) (TAM) (pavirNItye)   (naPRAva)
до угла. Там поверните направо.
to the corner. There you turn to the right.

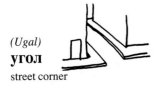

(Ugal)
угол
street corner

_____

(iDItye)   (DAL'she) (i) (PYErit) (VAmi)
Идите дальше и перед вами
Go a bit farther and in front of you

(BUdit)   (muZYEY)
будет музей.
will be the museum.

CAROLINE   **Спасибо.**

МИЛИЦИОНЕР   **Пожалуйста.**

(GDYE)   (MY)
Где мы?
Where are we?

(STOL)
стол _____
table

(KOSHka)
кошка
cat

Look at the words and phrases used in Russian to describe location. Write out each of these important little words. Notice that the noun for "table" has different endings according to the prepositions that precede it. You will not need to learn all of these endings. Pay closer attention to the highlighted forms.

(ZA) (staLOM)
за столом
behind

(PYErit) (staLOM)
перед столом
in front of

(NA) (staLYE)
на столе
on

_____

<table>
<tr><td>(U) (staLA)
у стола
next to</td><td></td><td>(Okala) (staLA)
около стола
near</td><td></td><td>(daliKO) (OT) (staLA
далеко от стол
far away</td><td></td></tr>
</table>

Now take a look at the **мальчик** (boy) and the **дом** (house). Can you write in the proper words to locate him?

1. _____   2. _____   3. _____

4. _____   5. _____   6. _____

(Eta)   (Ili)   (TO)

Это или то

This or that

You can do lots of things in Russian by using your finger to point and these two little words. Let's try it for fun. Fill in the blanks with the correct response.

(khaTItye)
1. **Вы хотите это или то?**   _____ , пожалуйста.
Would you like this one or that one?   This one, please.

(pritpachiTAitye)
2. **Вы предпочитаете это или то?**   _____ , пожалуйста.
Do you prefer this one or that one?   That one, please.

Нужные слова
(NUZHniye) *(slaVA)*

Necessary words

Write the Russian words in the space provided and say them aloud.

(kiNO)
кино
movie

(magaZIN)
магазин
store

(BANK)
банк
bank

(TSERkaf')
церковь
church

_____

_____

_____

_____

_____

(Ulitsa)
улица
street

(maSHYna)
машина
car

(apTYEka)
аптека
pharmacy

(kiOSK)
киоск
kiosk

_____

_____

_____

_____

Идти пешком
(iTI) *(pishKOM)*

Coming and going (on foot)

Russian verbs have endings to indicate who is performing the action. Remember back to the personal pronouns and look at the following table. Then write out the expressions in the blanks.
NOTE: Russians use the same word for "Coming" and "Going!"

я иду́	_____	I am going
ты идёшь	_____	you are going
он/она идёт	_____	he/she is going
мы идём	_____	we are going
вы идёте	_____	you are going
они иду́т	_____	they are going

(GDYE)   *(Ili)*   *(kuDA)*

Где или куда

Where or where to

We have already seen examples of the ending of a noun changing because of a preposition. We say the noun is in a specific *case*. The **nominative** (naming) case is the form of a noun found in dictionaries and word lists. Russian has six cases. To express location, Russians use the **prepositional or the accusative case**.

In answer to the question **«Где?»** ("Where?") Russians use the preposition **в** (in) or **на** (at) plus the **prepositional case**, which for most nouns has the ending **e**. This **e** is added to words that end in a consonant like **банк→банке**. For words that end in **a** or **я** or **o**, that letter is replaced by the **e**, **аптека→аптеке**.

Где мама? _____	**Она в магазине.** _____
Где папа? _____	**Он в банке.** _____
Где Иван? _____	**Он в аптеке.** _____
Где Ирина? _____	**Она на почте.** _____

In answer to the question **«Куда?»** ("Where to?"), Russians reply with the preposition **в** (in) or **на** (at) plus the **accusative case**. The accusative endings for masculine and neuter nouns are the same as the nominative. For feminine nouns, those that end in **a** will have the accusative case ending **y**, those ending in **я** will end in **ю**.

Куда идёт мама? _____	**Она идёт в магазин.** _____
Куда идёт папа? _____	**Он идёт в банк.** _____
Куда ты идёшь? _____	**Я иду в аптеку.** _____
Куда вы идёте? _____	**Мы идём на почту.** _____

That's an awful lot to learn. Go back over the section above and practice writing out in the spaces provided the new words and phrases. Then let's see if you can fill in the blanks on the next page.

1. **Папа и мама** _____ (GOrat) **в город.**
   are going

2. **Мама должна пойти** _____ (dalZHNA) .
   has to   go   to the bank.

3. **Папа** _____ **на почту.**
   is going

4. **Там** _____ (raBOtait) **работает Ирина.**
   at the post office   works

5. **Ирина и папа идут** _____ .
   to a store

6. **Мама уже** _____ .
   at the store.

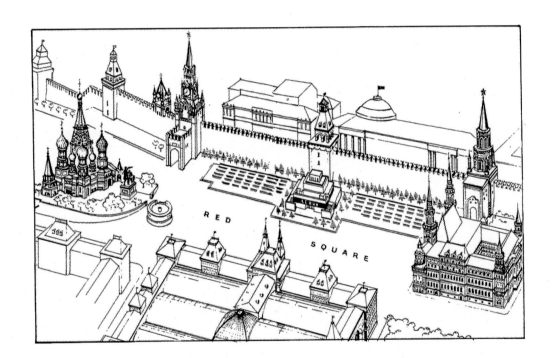

RED SQUARE

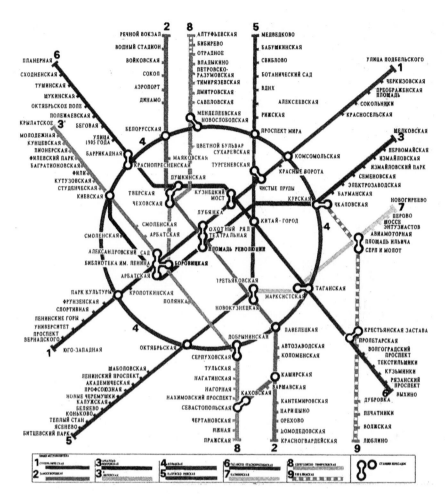

You will certainly want to use the public transportation systems in **Москва** or **Санкт-Петербург** (Saint Petersburg). The following dialogue contains some words and expressions you will find useful. Read the dialogue aloud several times to familiarize yourself with the meaning and pronunciation of the words. *And don't forget to take a ride on the **Метро**.*

CAROLINE

(paYEdim)   (takSI)
Поедем на такси   Let's ride in a taxi
(tiATR)
в театр.   to the theater.

MARK

(SLISHkam)   (DOraga)
Нет. Слишком дорого.   No. That's too expensive.

CAROLINE

Как насчёт метро?   How about the metro?
(uDOBna)   (BYStra)
Это удобно и быстро.   That's comfortable and quick.

MARK	*(nichiVO)* *(VIDna)* **Да. Но ничего не видно.**	Yes. But you can't see anything.
CAROLINE	*(YEdim)* *(afTObusye)* **Едем на автобусе?**	Should we take the bus?
MARK	*(priKRASna)* **Прекрасно! У тебя** *(biLYEty)* **есть билеты?**	Splendid! Do you have any tickets?
CAROLINE	*(kaNESHna)* **Конечно, у меня есть.**	Of course. I have some.

На автобусе (On the bus).

PASSENGER	*(vyKHOditye)* **Вы выходите?**	Are you getting off?
CAROLINE	*(SKAzhitye)* **Нет. Вы не скажете,** *(SKOL'ka)* *(astaNOvak)* **сколько остановок** **до Большого театра?**	No. Could you tell us, how many stops until the Bolshoi Theater?
PASSENGER	*(bal'SHOY)* *(CHEris)* **Большой театр через** **две остановки.**	The Bolshoi Theater comes after two stops.

After listening to the conversation above, you should be able to choose the correct answer and write it in the blank spaces.

1. **Поедем** _____ **в театр.**
   а. на автобусе   б. на метро   в. на такси

2. **Нет. Слишком** _____ .
   а. хорошо   б. дорого   в. дёшево

3. **Едем** _____ **автобусе?**
   а. на   б. через   в. в

4. **Вы** _____ ?
   а. скажете   б. едете   в. выходите

5. _____ **театр через две остановки.**
   а. Большой   б. наш   в. прекрасный

Fill in 1. b   2. б   3. а   4. в   5. а

36

Как мы едем?

(KAK) (MY) (YEdim)

How will we go?

Look at the pictures below, repeat the phrases, and then write them in the blanks.

(na) (taKSI)
на такси

_____

(afTObusye)
на автобусе

_____

(miTRO)
на метро

_____

(maSHYnye)
на машине

_____

Ехать

(YEkhat')

Coming and going (by vehicle)

Do you remember the Russian verb **идти** meaning to come or go **by foot**? Russians use another verb, **ехать**, if the act of coming or going takes place in a **car, bus, train, etc.**

я е́ду	_____	I am going
ты е́дешь	_____	you are going
она/он е́дет	_____	she/he is going
мы е́дем	_____	we are going
вы е́дете	_____	you are going
они е́дут	_____	they are going

(GDYE) (aNI) (kuDA) (aNI) (YEdut)

Где они? Куда они едут?

Where are they?   Where are they going?

(muSHYna)
Мужчина в Москве.
man

Мужчина едет в Москву.

(ZHENshyna)
Женщина в Вашингтоне.
woman

Женщина едет в Вашингтон.

(MAL'chik)
Мальчик в театре.
boy

Мальчик едет в театр.

(DYEvachka)
Девочка на балете.
little girl

Девочка едет на балет.

(malaDOY chilaVYEK)
Молодой человек в кино.*
young man

Молодой человек едет в кино.

(DYEvushka)
Девушка в Кремле.
girl/young lady

Девушка едет в Кремль.

---

*Some nouns in Russian that come from foreign words do not change their endings; they are what is called **indeclinable**: **кино**—movie theater/cinema, **кофе**—coffee, **кафе**—café.

38

(CHEY)   (CH'YA)   (CH'YO)   (CH'I)

Чей, Чья, Чьё, Чьи

Whose?

You already know that Russian nouns can be **masculine, feminine** and **neuter**, and **singular** or **plural**. Some modifiers must agree with the noun. In the chart below you will see that the words for "mine, your, our" change according to the noun. Russians say:

(MOY) (DOM) (maYA) (kvarTIra)   *(maYO) (pis'MO)*   *(maYI) (DYEti)*

мой дом, моя квартира, моё письмо, мои дети

my   house my   apartment   my   letter   my   children

ENGLISH	MASCULINE	FEMININE	NEUTER	ALL PLURALS
My	мой	моя	моё	мои
Your	твой	твоя	твоё	твои
Her/His	её/его	её/его	её/его	её/его
Our	наш	наша	наше	наши
Your	ваш	ваша	ваше	ваши
Their	их	их	их	их

See how well you can do in filling in the missing modifiers:

1. Это _____ кошка.
          my   cat

2. Это _____ улица.
          their   street

3. Это _____ собака.
          our   dog

4. Это _____ стол.
          her   table

5. Это _____ бабушка.
          your   grandmother

6. Это _____ банк.
          your (pl.)   bank

ANSWERS

Modifiers 1. моя 2. их 3. наша 4. её 5. твоя 6. ваш

39

7. Это _____ сын. **8.** Это _____ машина. **9.** Это _____ стул.

his son   my car   our chair

10. Это _____ яблоко. **11.** Это _____ дети. **12.** Это _____ дом.

your apple   her children   their house

Let's take a break. You've had a lot of information to absorb. See how much Russian you already know by trying your hand at the **кроссворд** (crossword).

По горизонтали

Across

1. They
3. Hotel
9. Policeman
10. Four
11. One
12. Museum

По вертикали

Down

2. No
4. Excuse me
5. Yes
6. Room/number
7. She
8. Five

40

(SKOL'ka)

Сколько?

How much/many?

The numbers are essential if you wish to get by in Russian. Do you remember the numbers from one to ten in Chapter 2? Say the words aloud and pay special attention to the stressed syllable. Let's cover them again and write them out for practice along with two new important words for telling time.

Number	Russian		Pronunciation
0	нуль	_____	*NUL'*
1	один	_____	*aDIN*
2	два	_____	*DVA*
3	три	_____	*TRI*
4	четыре	_____	*chiTYrye*
5	пять	_____	*PYAT'*
6	шесть	_____	*SHEST'*
7	семь	_____	*SYEM'*
8	восемь	_____	*VOsim'*
9	девять	_____	*DYEvit'*
10	десять	_____	*DYEsit'*
11	одиннадцать	_____	*aDInatsat'*
12	двенадцать	_____	*dviNAtsat'*

КОТОРЫЙ СЕЙЧАС ЧАС?

(kaTOry)   *(siyCHAS)*   *(CHAS)*

What time is it now?

Now you're ready to start telling time. Look at the clocks below.

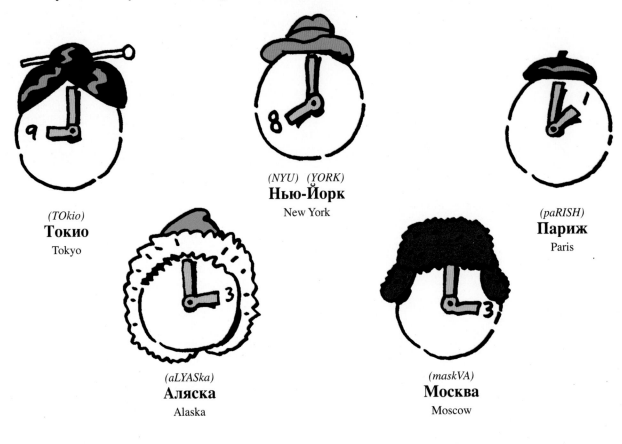

Токио
(TOkio)
Tokyo

Нью-Йорк
(NYU) (YORK)
New York

Париж
(paRISH)
Paris

Аляска
(aLYASka)
Alaska

Москва
(maskVA)
Moscow

В Токио	**На Аляске**	**В Нью-Йорке**	**В Москве**	**В Париже**
девять часов.	три часа.	восемь часов.	три часа.	час.

In order to express the time, Russians use the number plus a form of the word "hour"—**час**. For one o'clock, simply say **час** (*CHAS*). After the numbers two, three, and four, say **часа** (*chiSA*): **два часа, три часа, четыре часа**. After the number five and through twenty use **часов** (*chiSOF*): **пять часов, шесть часов, и т.д.**

Can you count around the clock? Try it just once. To add precision to your times you might want to add the words for "in the morning"—**утра** (*uTRA*), "in the afternoon"—**дня** (*DNYA*), "in the evening"—**вечера** (*VYEchira*).

ANSWERS

Clock час, два часа, три часа, четыре часа, пять часов, шесть часов, семь часов, восемь часов, девять часов, десять часов, одиннадцать часов, двенадцать часов.

42

Когда?

When?

Now that you can tell time, it's easy to tell someone *when* or *at what time* something will or did happen. You simply add the preposition **в** before the time. Tell when you are coming and then we'll fill in the blank!

Я приду в час.

_____

Я приду в три часа.

_____

Я приду в семь часов.

_____

Я приду в четыре часа.

_____

Я приду в десять часов.

_____

Now that we can get there on time, you'll want to learn the other important numbers. Notice that Russians make the words for eleven and twelve by adding one + ten—**один на десять = одиннадцать**, two + ten—**два на десять = двенадцать**. The same is true for the numbers from thirteen to nineteen. Once again, try to repeat them aloud and then write them in the blanks provided.

Number	Russian		Pronunciation
13	тринадцать	_____	*triNAtsat'*
14	четырнадцать	_____	*chiTYRnatsat'*
15	пятнадцать	_____	*pitNAtsat'*
16	шестнадцать	_____	*shistNAtsat'*
17	семнадцать	_____	*simNAtsat'*
18	восемнадцать	_____	*vasimNAtsat'*
19	девятнадцать	_____	*divitNAtsat'*

The numbers for twenty, thirty, fifty, sixty, seventy and eighty are really two tens—**два десять = двадцать**, three tens—**три десять = тридцать**, etc.

Number	Russian		Pronunciation
20	двадцать	_____	*DVAtsat'*
30	тридцать	_____	*TRItsat'*
40	сорок*	_____	*SOrak*
50	пятьдесят	_____	*pidiSYAT*
60	шестьдесят	_____	*shizdiSYAT*
70	семьдесят	_____	*SYEM'disit*
80	восемьдесят	_____	*VOsim'disit*

*The word **сорок** is an exception to the numbers. It comes from a word that used to mean a sack that held forty skins, a standard of measure for the number of skins needed to sew a fur coat in ancient Russia.

To make the numbers twenty-one, twenty-two, etc., just add the single digits from above.

21	22	23
двадцать один	**двадцать два**	**двадцать три**

24	25	26
двадцать четыре	**двадцать пять**	**двадцать шесть**

27	28	29
двадцать семь	**двадцать восемь**	**двадцать девять**

Here are all of the other numbers you'll need to know to get around completely. Be sure to practice them often, until you get the hang of it.

Number	Russian		Pronunciation
90	девяносто	_____	_diviNOSta_
100	сто	_____	_STO_
101	сто один	_____	_STO aDIN_
110	сто десять	_____	_STO DYEsit'_
200	двести	_____	_DVYESti_
300	триста	_____	_TRISta_
400	четыреста	_____	_chiTYrista_
500	пятьсот	_____	_pit'SOT_
600	шестьсот	_____	_shist'SOT_
700	семьсот	_____	_sim'SOT_
800	восемьсот	_____	_vasim'SOT_
900	девятьсот	_____	_divit'SOT_
1000	тысяча	_____	_TYsicha_
2000	две тысячи	_____	_DVYE TYsichi_
5000	пять тысяч	_____	_PYAT' TYsich_
1.000.000	миллион	_____	_miliON_
2.000.000	два миллиона	_____	_DVA miliOna_
5.000.000	пять миллионов	_____	_PYAT' miliOnaf_
1.000.000.000	миллиард	_____	_miliART_

Instead of commas to distinguish thousands, millions, etc., Russians use a period or a simple space: 1.000.000.000 or 1 000 000 000. Russians use a comma to indicate the period in decimals: 1,3 is the Russian way of identifying 1.3 (one and three tenths or one point three).

Ordinal Numbers

The ordinal numbers in Russian for **first, second, third**, etc. are modifiers, and they will have different endings depending upon the gender of the noun: first floor—**первый этаж**, second cat—**вторая кошка**, fifth window—**пятое окно**.

Write in the floors in the elevator by hand in the spaces provided and say them aloud.

(diVYAty)
девятый
ninth

_____

(sid'MOY)
седьмой
seventh

_____

(PYAty)
пятый
fifth

_____

(TRYEti)
третий
third

_____

(PYERvy)
первый
first

_____

ВЫЗОВ СТОП

(diSYAty)
десятый
tenth

_____

(vas'MOY)
восьмой
eighth

_____

(shiSTOY)
шестой
sixth

_____

(chitVYORty)
четвертый
fourth

_____

(ftaROY)
второй
second

_____

Sometimes, especially in plane and train schedules, Russians use the 24-hour clock, so that the numbers from 13 to 24 designate the P.M. hours.

| One o'clock P.M. | = | **Тринадцать часов.** | *(triNATsat' chiSOF)* |

In addition to saying twelve o'clock, **двенадцать часов**, Russians can say

Noon	**Полдень** *(POLdyen')*	*or*	Midnight	**Полночь** *(POLnach)*

Once an hour has begun, Russians look forward to the next hour. Thus 1:05 is five minutes of
the second hour. They also make use of these two useful quantities for a quarter: **четверть**, *(CHETvirt')* and
a half: **половина**. *(palaVIna)*

(PYAT) (miNUT) (ftaROva)
пять минут второго

(DYEsit') (miNUT) (TRYEt'yiva)
десять минут третьего

(CHETvirt') (chitVYORtava)
четверть четвёртого

(DVAtsat') (miNUT) (PYAtava)
двадцать минут пятого

(DVAtsat') (PYAT')(miNUT) (shiSTOva)
двадцать пять минут шестого

(palaVIna) (sid'MOva)
половина седьмого

After the half hour Russians count backwards; thus 7:35 is the eighth hour minus twenty-five minutes.

(byez) (dvatsaTI) (piTI) (VOsim')
без двадцати пяти восемь

(byez) (dvatsaTI) (DYEvit')
без двадцати девять

(byez) (CHETvirti) (DYEsit')
без четверти десять

(byez) (disiTI) (aDInatsat')

без десяти одиннадцать

(byez) (piTI) (dviNAtsat')

без пяти двенадцать

Can you give a set of numbers around the clock. Try to say the following times. Then answer the question, **который сейчас час?** Fill in the blanks.

а. 1:00 _____

б. 2:05 _____

в. 3:10 _____

г. 4:15 _____

д. 5:20 _____

е. 6:25 _____

ё. 7:30 _____

ж. 8:35 _____

з. 9:40 _____

и. 10:45 _____

й. 11:50 _____

к. 12:55 _____

Let's watch Mark in the following encounter. Look over the text and then repeat the dialogue several times until you are comfortable with all the highlighted words and phrases.

MARK	**Извините, пожалуйста.**	Excuse me.
	(kaTOry) *(siCHAS)* **Который сейчас час?**	What time is it?
ГОСПОДИН	**Уже полночь.**	It's already midnight.
MARK	*(MOzhit)* *(BYT')* **Не может быть!**	That can't be!
	(SONtse) *(SVYEtit)* **Солнце светит.**	The sun is shining.
ГОСПОДИН	*(PRAvy)* **Вы правы.**	You're right.
	Тогда, уже полдень.	Then, it's noon.
MARK	*(SHUtitye)* **Вы шутите?**	Are you joking?
ГОСПОДИН	**Нет. Но мои часы**	No. But my watch
	(raBOtayut) **не работают.**	isn't working.
	(tuRIST) **Вы турист?**	Are you a tourist?
MARK	**Да, конечно.**	Yes, of course.
ГОСПОДИН	*(kuPIT')* **Вы хотите купить**	Do you want to by a
	часы?	watch?
MARK	*(STOyat)* **Сколько они стоят?**	How much do they cost?
	(TOL'ka) **У меня только**	I only have
	тысяча рублей.	a thousand rubles.
ГОСПОДИН	**Эти часы стоят**	This watch costs
	пятьсот рублей.	five hundred rubles.
MARK	*(vaz'MU)* **Хорошо. Я возьму.**	Fine. I'll take it.

Note: Did you notice how the word for "watch" (**часы**) is related to the word for hour **час**. Actually, the word for "watch" is made from a plural of "hours."

Can you write these phrases from the dialogue in Russian?

1. What time is it? _____

2. It's already midnight. _____

3. But my watch isn't working. _____

4. Do you want to buy a watch? _____

(kaKOY)   *(siVOdnya)*   *(DYEN')*

КАКОЙ СЕГОДНЯ ДЕНЬ?

What day is today?

(paniDYEL'nik)	*(FTORnik)*	*(sriDA)*	*(chitVYERK)*	*(PYATnitsa)*	*(suBOta)*	*(vaskriSYEn'ye)*
понедельник	вторник	среда	четверг	пятница	суббота	воскресенье

(siVOdnya)
сегодня
today

(fchiRA)
вчера
yesterday

(ZAFtra)
завтра
tomorrow

(uZHE)
уже
already

(yiSCHO)
ещё
still

(aPYAT')
опять
again

If you want to say when (on what day) you are coming, use the preposition **в** and the **accusative case**. Read the answers to the question:

When do you work?	**Когда вы работаете?**	*(kagDA) (VY) (raBOtaitye)*

ANSWERS

Dialogue 1. Который сейчас час? 2. Уже полночь. 3. Но мои часы не работают. 4. Вы хотите купить часы?

I work	**Я работаю**	
on Monday	**в понедельник.**	*(f) (paniDYEL'nik)*
on Tuesday	**во вторник.**	*(va) (FTORnik)*
on Wednesday	**в среду.**	*(f) (SRYEdu)*
on Thursday	**в четверг.**	*(f) (chitVYERK)*
on Friday	**в пятницу.**	*(f) (PYATnitsu)*
I don't work	**Я не работаю**	
on Saturday	**в субботу.**	*(f) (suBOtu)*
on Sunday	**в воскресенье.**	*(v) (vaskriSYEn'ye)*

Did you notice that the days of the week are not capitalized in Russian? Pay attention also to the form **во вторник**.

Can you match up the following days of the week and adverbs of time with their English equivalents?

1.	**сегодня**	а.	tomorrow
2.	**вторник**	б.	already
3.	**завтра**	в.	Wednesday
4.	**среда**	г.	yesterday
5.	**уже**	д.	again
6.	**вчера**	е.	Tuesday
7.	**опять**	ё.	today

(RUskiye)   *(glaGOly)*
РУССКИЕ ГЛАГОЛЫ
Russian verbs

You have already seen the personal pronouns for I, you, he, etc. and the conjugation of the Russian verbs for motion on foot (**идти**) and by vehicle (**ехать**). Russian verbs belong to one of two classes or **conjugations** in the present tense. Look at the endings for the **first conjugation**.

Note how the forms change according to the subject of the sentence.

PRONOUN	VERB		VERB	
	рабóтать	(to work)	**жить**	(to live)
я	**рабóтаю**	(I work)	**живý**	(I live)
ты	**рабóтаешь**	(you work)	**живёшь**	(you live)
он/она	**рабóтает**	(she/he works)	**живёт**	(she/he lives)
мы	**рабóтаем**	(we work)	**живём**	(we live)
вы	**рабóтаете**	(you work)	**живёте**	(you live)
они	**рабóтают**	(they work)	**живýт**	(they live)

The endings vary slightly according to whether they come after a consonant or a vowel, and whether or not they are stressed.

You can form lots of verbs based on the chart above. Here are just a few examples:

ENGLISH	RUSSIAN INFINITIVE	CONJUGATED FORM
to rest	*(adyKHAT')* **отдыхать**	*(YA) (adyKHAyu)* **я отдыхаю**
to have breakfast	*(ZAFtrakat')* **завтракать**	*(TY) (ZAFtrakaish)* **ты завтракаешь**
to have lunch/dinner	*(aBYEdat')* **обедать**	*(aNA) (aBYEdait)* **она обедает**
to know	*(ZNAT')* **знать**	*(ON) (ZNAit)* **он знает**
to have supper	*(Uzhinat')* **ужинать**	*(MY) (Uzhinaim)* **мы ужинаем**
to be late	*(aPAZdyvat')* **опаздывать**	*(VY) (aPAZdyvaitye)* **вы опаздываете**
to understand	*(paniMAT')* **понимать**	*(aNI) (paniMAyut)* **они понимают**

Now try your own hand in writing in the correct endings of these verbs.

1. I understand.   **Я понима** _____ .

2. We are resting.   **Мы отдыха** _____ .

3. They are breakfasting. **Они завтрака** _____ .

4. She is dining.   **Она обеда** _____ .

5. Don't you know?   **Вы не зна** _____ ?

It's time to stop and catch our breath. We already know a tremendous amount as the little narrative below will indicate. Just fill in the blanks with the proper verbal endings, and then try writing out a quick translation to indicate how much you've already mastered.

Вера и Андрей жив _____ **в Москве. Они завтрака** _____ **в семь часов**
                       live   breakfast

утра. Андрей работа _____ **в Кремле и он ед** _____ **туда на метро.**
                        works   goes   there

Вера работа _____ **на почте и утром она ид** _____ **пешком на почту.**
         works   post office   goes   on foot

Сегодня она опаздыва _____ **и она ед** _____ **на такси. Вечером Вера**
Today   is late   goes   In the evening

спрашива _____ **, «Где мы ужина** _____ **?» Андрей не хочет ужинать в**
      asks   supper   want   to have supper

ресторане, и отвеча _____ **«Я не зна** _____ **, где ты**
restaurant   replies   know

ужина _____ **, но я сегодня вечером отдыха** _____ **.».**
   supper   rest

Train Service

Traveling by train can be a pleasant way to travel between cities in Russia and to catch a glimpse of the countryside and the people. The overnight trains between **Москва** and **Санкт-Петербург** provide a reliable and comfortable opportunity to make acquaintants, avoid weather delays at airports, and get a good night's sleep. In Moscow there are several train stations depending upon your destination. Be sure to ask from which station your train departs.

The following dialogue contains important words and phrases connected with train travel. Read it aloud several times.

MARK	*(vagZAlye)* **Вот мы на вокзале.**	Here we are at the station.
STEFANIE	**Папа, мы едем на** *(KRASnoy)* *(striLYE)* **«Красной стреле»** **в Санкт-Петербург?**	Dad, are we riding on the "Red Arrow" to Saint Petersburg?
MARK	**Да.** (to the clerk) *(aBRATny)* **Сколько стоит обратный** *(bilYET)* **билет в Санкт-Петербург?**	Yes. How much does a round-trip ticket to Petersburg cost?
ДЕВУШКА (clerk)	**Билет в мягком вагоне?**	A first class ticket? (in the soft car)
MARK	*(CHETvira)* **Да. Нас четверо.**	Yes. There are four of us.

ДЕВУШКА	*(NUZHna)* **Вам нужно одно или** *(kuPYE)* **два купе. Это будет** *(ruBLYEY)* **5000 или 7000 рублей.**	You'll need one or two compartments. That will be 5000 or 7000 rubles.
MARK	*(kuPIravanam)* *(vaGOnye)* **А в купированном вагоне?**	And in a sleeping car?
ДЕВУШКА	**3500 рублей.**	3500 rubles.
MARK	*(atpraVLYAitsa)* **Когда отправляется** **поезд?**	When does the train depart?
ДЕВУШКА	**В 23:45**	At 11:45 P.M. (23:45).
MARK	*(platFORmy)* **С какой платформы?**	From which platform?
ДЕВУШКА	**Платформа № 4.**	Track #4.
	Вот ваши билеты.	Here are your tickets.
STEFANIE	*(misTA)* **Папа, где наши места?**	Dad, where are our places?
MARK	**Вагон 10, места 5-8.**	Car 10, seats 5–8.

You might find yourself on all sorts of trains. The famous Trans-Siberian Railway can be the adventure of a lifetime. Traveling out to or back from a country **дача** (dacha—villa) you might take an Express train (**Скорый поезд**). For overnight trains, as Mark and his daughter, Stefanie, have just learned, there are several categories of service for comfort. In first class (**мягкий вагон**) you can have a compartment (**купе**) with two very comfortable beds or with four beds. There is also the regular sleeping car (**купированный вагон**).

Try reading aloud the names of some of Moscow's favorite train stations. Then see if you can pair them with their English equivalents.

1. **Казанский вокзал.**
2. **Киевский вокзал.**
3. **Белорусский вокзал.**
4. **Рижский вокзал.**
5. **Ярославский вокзал.**

a. Riga Station
б. Yaroslav Station
в. Kazan Station
г. Kiev Station
д. Byelorussian Station

ANSWERS

Train stations 1. в 2. г 3. д 4. а 5. б

Look at the following schedule for departures from **Москва Ярославская** (Moscow Yaroslav Station). From here trains depart for Siberia and the Far East. You can go travel to **Владивосток** (Vladivostok) or **Хабаровск** (Khabarovsk), and, of course, **Ярославль** (Yaroslavl). On the time schedule note the words **Расписание** (Schedule), **Отправление** (departure), **Пункт отправления** (Point of Departure), and **Пункт прибытия** (Point of Arrival).

Расписание по станции МОСКВА ЯРОСЛАВСКАЯ - отправление

№	Пункт отправления	Пункт прибытия	Отправление
674	МОСКВА ЯРОСЛАВСКАЯ	КИНЕШМА	00:20
240	МОСКВА ЯРОСЛАВСКАЯ	ВЛАДИВОСТОК	00:35
044	МОСКВА ЯРОСЛАВСКАЯ	ХАБАРОВСК	00:35
044	МОСКВА ЯРОСЛАВСКАЯ	ВЛАДИВОСТОК	00:35
044	МОСКВА ЯРОСЛАВСКАЯ	СОВЕТСК.ГАВАНЬ-СОРТ.	00:35
044	МОСКВА ЯРОСЛАВСКАЯ	УЛАН-УДЕ ПАСС	00:35
918	МОСКВА ЯРОСЛАВСКАЯ	ВЛАДИВОСТОК	01:01
904	МОСКВА ЯРОСЛАВСКАЯ	ВЛАДИВОСТОК	05:20
828	МОСКВА ЯРОСЛАВСКАЯ	ЯРОСЛАВЛЬ-ГЛАВНЫЙ	08:24
016	МОСКВА ЯРОСЛАВСКАЯ	АРХАНГЕЛЬСК ГОРОД	09:35
376	МОСКВА ЯРОСЛАВСКАЯ	ВОРКУТА	12:30
376	МОСКВА ЯРОСЛАВСКАЯ	ЛАБЫТНАНГИ	12:30
350	МОСКВА ЯРОСЛАВСКАЯ	БЛАГОВЕЩЕНСК	13:35
340	МОСКВА ЯРОСЛАВСКАЯ	ЧИТА 2	13:35
034	МОСКВА ЯРОСЛАВСКАЯ	СОСНОГОРСК	14:05
028	МОСКВА ЯРОСЛАВСКАЯ	СЫКТЫВКАР	14:05
024	МОСКВА ЯРОСЛАВСКАЯ	СЫКТЫВКАР	14:05
034	МОСКВА ЯРОСЛАВСКАЯ	СЫКТЫВКАР	14:05

Can you answer a few of these questions?

1. When does the first train to Khabarovsk leave?
2. When is the morning train to Yaroslavl?
3. How many trains are there to Vladivostok?
4. Is there a train to Archangelsk and when?

ANSWERS

Questions 1. 0:35 (12:35 AM) **2.** 8:24 AM **3.** Four (two at 0:35, 1:01, 5:20) **4.** Yes. At 9:35 AM.

ПОЕЗД

Train

(putiSHESTvavat')
путешествовать
to travel

(pasaZHYR)
пассажир
passenger

(saDItsa)
садиться
to sit down

(staYAT')
стоять
to stand

(ZAL azhiyDAniya)
зал ожидания
waiting lounge

(platFORma)
платформа
platform

(pravadNIK)
проводник
conductor

ПСКОВ
РОСТОВ
НОВГОРОД
СМОЛЕНСК

(raspiSAniye)
расписание
schedule

(tiLYESHka)
тележка
luggage cart

(naSIL'schik)
носильщик
porter

The Possessive Modifiers

(MOY)	(TVOY)	(yiVO)	(yiYO)	(NASH')	(VASH)	(IKH)

Мой, твой, его, её, наш, ваш, их

my	your	his	her	our	your	their

On your journey you will certainly need to know how to distinguish your own belongings from those of others. Just as we use "my, your, his, her, our, their" in English, remember that Russians too have a way of expressing possession. The easiest category is the third person, "he, she and their," for which Russians use **его, её, их.**

This is his train and seat.	Это его поезд и место.
This is her train and seat.	Это её поезд и место.
This is their train and seat.	Это их поезд и место.

The forms for **его, её, их** remain unchanged regardless of the noun.

Remember that we have already seen that when we want to say "my, your, or our," the Russian word changes according to the gender of the noun. Look at the chart below.

  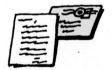

Это	**мой** стул	**моя** газета	**моё** письмо	**мои** книги
Это	**твой** стул	**твоя** газета	**твоё** письмо	**твои** книги
Это	**наш** стул	**наша** газета	**наше** письмо	**наши** книги
Это	**ваш** стул	**ваша** газета	**ваше** письмо	**ваши** книги

Caroline is having some trouble with her seats on the train. Can you help her fill in the blanks?

Извините, пожалуйста. Это _____ место? _____ места,
                                              your   seat   Our   seats

номера 12, 13, 14, 15.

Да, это _____ место, номер 12. Нет, нет _____ место,
              my   my

номер 19. Это _____ места.
                        your

Марк, это _____ место. Где Стефании и Александр?
                    your

Это _____ место, и это _____ место.
          her   his

(STRAny)   *(i)* *(yizyKI)*

Страны и языки
Countries and Languages

Now let's examine how Russians look at the rest of the world and learn how to say the names of the different countries in Russian. First look at the map and then match the Russian names with their English counterparts.

(kantiNYENty)   *(i)*   *(STRAny)*

Континенты и страны
Continents and countries

Africa	*(AFrika)* **Африка**	Asia	*(Aziya)* **Азия**	
America	*(aMYErika)* **Америка**	Australia	*(afSTRAliya)* **Австралия**	
Central America	*(tsenTRAL'naya)* *(aMYErika)* **Центральная Америка**	Europe	*(yiVROpa)* **Европа**	
North America	*(SVEvirnaya)* *(aMYErika)* **Северная Америка**	1. Canada	*(kaNAda)* **Канада**	
South America	*(YUZHnaya)* *(aMYErika)* **Южная Америка**	2. United States	*(sayidiNYOniye)* *(SHTaty)* **Соединённые Штаты**	

1. Канада
2. Соединённые Штаты

3. Austria	*(AFstriya)* **Австрия**	13. Italy	*(iTAliya)* **Италия**
4. Belgium	*(BYEL'giya)* **Бельгия**	14. Norway	*(narVYEgiya)* **Норвегия**
5. Bulgaria	*(balGAriya)* **Болгария**	15. Poland	*(POL'sha)* **Польша**
6. Denmark	*(DAniya)* **Дания**	16. Portugal	*(partuGAliya)* **Португалия**
7. England	*(ANgliya)* **Англия**	17. Romania	*(ruMYniya)* **Румыния**
8. France	*(FRANtsiya)* **Франция**	18. Scotland	*(shatLANdiya)* **Шотландия**
9. Germany	*(girMAniya)* **Германия**	19. Slovenia	*(slaVEniya)* **Словения**
10. Greece	*(GREtsiya)* **Греция**	20. Spain	*(iSPAniya)* **Испания**
11. Hungary	*(VYENgriya)* **Венгрия**	21. Sweden	*(SHVYEtsiya)* **Швеция**
12. Ireland	*(irLANdiya)* **Ирландия**	22. Switzerland	*(shviyTSAriya)* **Швейцария**

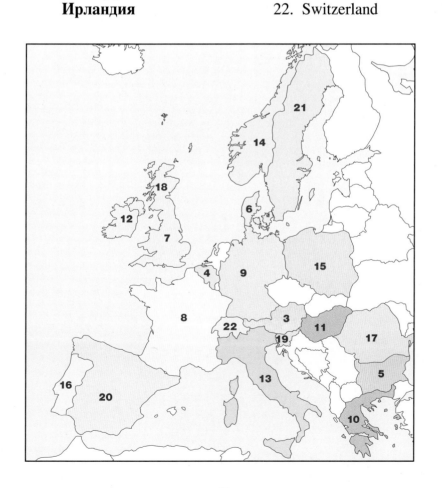

23. Azerbaijan	*(azirbayDZHAN)* **Азербайджан**	30. Kazakhstan	*(kazakhSTAN)* **Казахстан**
24. Belarus	*(bilaRUS')* **Беларусь**	31. Latvia	*(LATviya)* **Латвия**
25. China	*(kiTAY)* **Китай**	32. Mongolia	*(manGOliya)* **Монголия**
26. Estonia	*(eSTOniya)* **Эстония**	33. North Korea	*(SEvirnaya kaREya)* **Северная Корея**
27. Finland	*(finLYANdiya)* **Финляндия**	34. Russia	*(raSIya)* **Россия**
28. Georgia	*(GRUziya)* **Грузия**	35. Ukraine	*(ukraIna)* **Украина**
29. Japan	*(yaPOniya)* **Япония**		

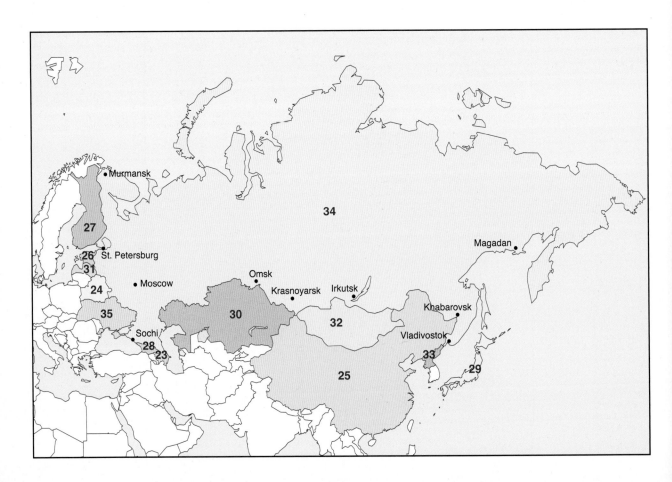

(natsiaNAL'nasti)

Национальности

Nationalities

It is very easy to tell someone your nationality in Russian. Simply use the pronoun **Я** and the proper masculine or feminine form:

(RUski)		*(RUskaya)*
Я русский.	I'm a Russian.	**Я русская.**

MASCULINE	ENGLISH	FEMININE
(azirbayDZHAnits) **Я азербайджанец.**	I'm Azerbaijanian.	*(azirbayDZHANka)* **Я азербайджанка.**
(amiriKAnits) **Я американец.**	I'm American.	*(amiriKANka)* **Я американка.**
(armiNIN) **Я армянин.**	I'm Armenian.	*(arMYANka)* **Я армянка.**
(afstraLIyits) **Я австралиец.**	I'm Australian.	*(afstraLIYka)* **Я австралийка.**
(angliCHAnin) **Я англичанин.**	I'm British.	*(angliCHANka)* **Я англичанка.**
(bilaRUS) **Я беларус.**	I'm Belarussian.	*(bilaRUSka)* **Я беларуска.**
(kaNAdits) **Я канадец.**	I'm Canadian.	*(kaNATka)* **Я канадка.**
(eSTOnits) **Я эстонец.**	I'm Estonian.	*(eSTONka)* **Я эстонка.**
(gruZIN) **Я грузин.**	I'm Georgian.	*(gruZINka)* **Я грузинка.**
(kaZAKH) **Я казах.**	I'm Kazakh.	*(kaZASHka)* **Я казашка.**
(kyrGYS) **Я кыргыз.**	I'm Kyrgyzian.	*(kyrGYSka)* **Я кыргызка.**

63

(laTYSH)
Я латыш.

I'm Latvian.

(laTYSHka)
Я латышка.

(liTOvits)
Я литовец.

I'm Lithuanian.

(liTOFka)
Я литовка.

(maldaVAnin)
Я молдованин.

I'm Moldovian.

(maldaVANka)
Я молдованка.

(taDZHIK)
Я таджик.

I'm Tajik.

(taDHICHka)
Я таджичка.

(turkMYEN)
Я туркмен.

I'm Turkmenian.

(turkMYENka)
Я туркменка.

(ukraInits)
Я украинец.

I'm Ukrainian.

(ukraINka)
Я украинка.

(uzBYEK)
Я узбек.

I'm Uzbek.

(uzBYECHka)
Я узбечка.

(YA)   *(gavaRYU)*   *(pa-RUski)*

Я говорю по-русски.
I speak Russian.

(gavaRIT')

You already know the first conjugation of Russian verbs. The verb **говорить** (to speak) belongs to the second conjugation. Look at the Russian forms for this verb and another second

(spiSHYT')

conjugation verb meaning "to hurry"—**спешить**.

Pronoun	Russian Verb	English	Russian Verb	English
	говорить		**спешить**	
я	**говорю́**	I speak	**спешу́**	I am hurrying
ты	**говори́шь**	you speak	**спеши́шь**	you are hurrying
она/он	**говори́т**	she/he speaks	**спеши́т**	she/he is hurrying
мы	**говори́м**	we speak	**спеши́м**	we are hurrying
вы	**говори́те**	you speak	**спеши́те**	you are hurrying
они	**говоря́т**	they speak	**спеша́т**	they are hurrying

Note how the endings vary slightly according to a spelling rule in Russian which states that after **ш, щ, ч, ж** and **ч**, you may not write **я** or **ю** but must substitute for them the letters **a** and **y**.

To say "I speak Russian" use the form **Я говорю по-русски.**

How would you ask "Do you speak Russian?" _____

This form—**по-русски** or **по-английски** (English)—is useful in a variety of expressions concerning language ability. You can combine the language you want to describe with the Russian verbs: **Я понимаю** (I understand), **Я читаю** (I read), and **Я пишу** (I write).

Now it's your turn to say the Russian sentences aloud and then practice writing them in the spaces below. Can you figure out the meanings for all of the sentences?

1. **Они говорят по-русски.** _____

2. **Она говорит по-русски.** _____

3. **Мы говорим по-английски.** _____

4. **Ты понимаешь по-русски?** _____

5. **Он читает по-английски.** _____

6. **Вы читаете по-русски?** _____

7. **Она говорит по-английски.** _____

8. **Я говорю по-французски.** _____

9. **Они понимают по-испански.** _____

10. **Они говорят по-украински.** _____

ANSWERS

Do you speak Russian? Вы говорите по-русски?

Speaking 1. They speak Russian. 2. She speaks Russian. 3. We speak English. 4. Do you understand Russian? 5. She reads English. 6. Do you read Russian? 7. She speaks English. 8. I speak French. 9. They understand Spanish. 10. They speak Ukrainian.

65

(RUskiye) *(imiNA)*

Русские имена

Russian names

Russians have three names: a first name, **имя**; a patronymic derived from one's father's name, **отчество**; and a family name, **фамилия**. The polite way to refer to recent acquaintances is with the name and patronymic: for example, Boris Nikolaevich—**Борис Николаевич** (*baRIS nikaLAyivich*) or Anna Petrovna—**Анна Петровна** (*Ana piTROVna*). When Russians use their first names, they are likely to have a nickname; for example, Ivan—**Иван** becomes Vanya—**Ваня**, Aleksandr—**Александр** becomes Sasha—**Саша**.

(YA) *(patiRYAla)* *(maYU)* *(SUMku)*

Я потеряла мою сумку.

I've lost my purse.

Caroline has lost her purse while out sightseeing. She approaches a policeman for help.

CAROLINE

(izviNItye)

Извините, пожалуйста. — Excuse me please.

Вы говорите по-английски? — Do you speak English?

МИЛИЦИОНЕР (Policeman)	*(niMNOga)* **Только немного.**	Just a little.
CAROLINE	*(MOzhitye)* *(paMOCH)* **Вы можете мне помочь?**	Can you help me?
МИЛИЦИОНЕР	*(kaNYESHna)* *(sluCHIlas')* **Конечно. Что случилось?**	Of course. What happened?
CAROLINE	**Я потеряла мою сумку.**	I've lost my purse.
МИЛИЦИОНЕР	**Ваша сумка? Как? Где?**	Your purse? How? Where?
CAROLINE	*(ZNAyu)* *(byLA)* **Я не знаю. Я была в** *(DYElat')* **метро. Что мне делать?**	I don't know. I was on the metro. What should I do?
МИЛИЦИОНЕР	*(BYla)* **Что было в сумке?**	What was in the purse?
CAROLINE	*(PASpart)* *(VIza)* **Мой паспорт, виза,** *(buMAZHnik)* **и бумажник.**	My passport, visa, and wallet.
МИЛИЦИОНЕР	**Что ещё?**	What else?
CAROLINE	**Кредитные карточки и** *(daROZHniye)* *(CHEki)* **дорожные чеки.**	Credit cards and travelers' checks.
МИЛИЦИОНЕР	*(pazvaNItye)* *(byuRO)* **Позвоните в бюро** *(naKHOdak)* **находок.**	Call the Lost and Found Office.
CAROLINE	*(saVYET)* **Спасибо за совет.**	Thanks for the advice.
МИЛИЦИОНЕР	*(zhiLAyu)* **Не за что. Желаю вам** *(uSPEkha)* **успеха.**	Don't mention it. I wish you success.
CAROLINE	**До свидания.**	Goodbye.

You should have noticed several verbs indicating actions that were done in the past: I lost—**я потеряла**, I was—**я была**, What was—**Что было**. The **past tense** in Russian is formed by dropping the **ть** from the infinitive verb form and adding **л** for a masculine subject, **ла** for a female subject, **ло** for a neuter subject, and **ли** for any plural subject.

8 | *(na)* *(daROgye)*
На дороге
On the Road

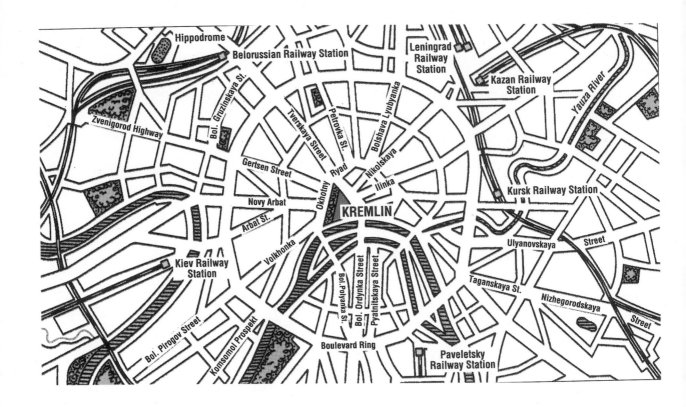

(VZYAT') *(napraKAT)* *(maSHYnu)*
ВЗЯТЬ НАПРОКАТ МАШИНУ
Renting a car

To reserve a car for rental you might want to contact your travel bureau in advance. You can also rent a car at the major tourist hotels in Russia. Rates vary according to the car you choose and there will be a charge for rental including insurance, plus a mileage charge. You need a valid driver's license.

Mark has decided that he can get around and see more of the city with his family if he rents a car. Let's see how he goes about renting a car for the week.

MARK	*(khaTYEL)* Доброе утро. Я хотел бы взять на прокат машину.	Good morning. I would like to rent a car.
ДЕВУШКА (Young Woman)	*(DYEN')* Пожалуйста. На один день?	Certainly. For one day?
MARK	Нет, на одну неделю.	No, for one week.

68

ДЕВУШКА	*(pritpachiTAitye)* **Вы предпочитаете** *(MAlin'kuyu)* *(bal'SHUyu)* **маленькую или большую** **машину?**	Do you prefer a small or a large car?
MARK	*(mikraafTObus)* **Нам нужен микроавтобус.**	We need a minivan.
ДЕВУШКА	*(praBLYEma)* **Это не проблема.**	That's no problem.
MARK	*(binZIN)* *(FKHOdit)* *(STOimast')* **Бензин входит в стоимость?**	Is gas included in the price?
ДЕВУШКА	*(kuPIt')* **Нет, но можно купить** *(lyuBOY)* *(binzakaLONkye)* **на любой бензоколонке.**	No, but you can buy it at any service station.
MARK	*(vaDItil'skiye)* *(praVA)* **Вот мои водительские права.**	Here is my driver's license.
ДЕВУШКА	*(kriDITnaya)* **У вас есть кредитная** *(KARtachka)* **карточка?**	Do you have a credit card?
MARK	**Конечно. Вот она.**	Of course. Here it is.
ДЕВУШКА	*(shasLIvava)* *(puTI)* **Счастливого пути!**	Have a good trip!

Pretend that you want to rent a car. Can you do it? Try to fill in the blanks below with the correct words or expressions.

1. Я хотел бы _____ машину.

2. Нам нужен _____ .

3. Вот мои _____ права.

4. _____ входит в стоимость?

ДОРОЖНЫЕ ЗНАКИ

(daROZHniye) *(ZNaki)*

Road signs

If you're planning to drive while you're abroad, it's important to spend some time memorizing the meanings of these signs.

Главная дорога

Right of Way

Опасность

Danger

Стоп

Stop

Максимальная скорость

Maximum Speed

Минимальная скорость

Minimum Speed

Конец ограничения

End of Speed Limit

Въезд запрещен

No Entrance

Уступите дорогу

Yield Right of Way

Двустороннее движение

Two-Way Traffic

Опасный поворот

Dangerous Curve

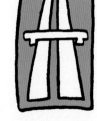

Автомагистраль

Expressway

Конец автомагистрали

End of Expressway

Таможня

Customs

Обгон запрещён

No Passing

**Конец зоны
запрещения обгона**

End No Passing Zone

Одностороннее движение

One-way Traffic

Объезд

Detour

Движение запрещёно

Road Closed

(Traffic Prohibited)

Стоянка

Parking

Остановка запрещена

No Standing

Круговое движение

Roundabout

Место для разворота

Place for U-turn

Стоянка запрещена

No Parking

Велосипеды запрещены

Bicycles Prohibited

Пешеходный переход

Pedestrian Crossing

**Железнодорожный
переезд без
шлагбаума**

Railroad Crossing

(No Gate)

**Железнодорожный
переезд со
шлагбаумом**

Railroad Crossing

(With Gate)

БЕНЗОКОЛОНКА

The service station

Gasoline is sold by the liter in Russia. There may be several grades of gasoline available indicated by octane. The most popular seem to be A90 or 92 for Regular and Аи95 for Super. You should have no problem locating a station, but nowadays you can always search the internet for **Бензоколонки в Москве.** Most Europeans have a good idea of how many liters of gasoline they use per 100 kilometers. If you want to be safe, try to calculate your own mileage in the city and on the open road.

MARK	*(LItrav)* **Сорок литров, пожалуйста.**	Forty liters, please.
CASHIER	*(diviNOsta)* *(ftoROva)* **Девяносто второго** *(PYAtava)* **или девяносто пятого?**	Regular (92 octane) or super (95 octane)?
MARK	**Девяносто пятого.** *(praVYER'tye)* **Проверьте, пожалуйста** *(masla)* *(VOdu)* *(SHYny)* **масло, воду и шины.**	Super (95 octane). Please check the oil, water, and tires.
CASHIER	**Всё в порядке.**	Everything's in order.
MARK	*(aftadaROZHnaya)* **У вас есть автодорожная** *(KARta)* **карта? Как проехать** *(aftaSYERvis)* **в автосервис?**	Do you have a road map? How do we get to the repair shop?
CASHIER	**Прямо десять километров,** **а потом на право.**	Straight ahead 10 kilometers, and then to the right.
MARK	**Спасибо. До свидания.**	Thank you. Good-bye.

(fpiRYOT)
вперёд
forward

(naLYEva)
налево
left

(naPRAva)
направо
right

(naZAT)
назад
backward

(SYEvir)
север
north

(ZApat)
запад
west

(vaSTOK)
восток
east

(YUK)
юг
south

(avtamaBIL')
(maSHYna)

АВТОМОБИЛЬ - МАШИНА

Automobile   Car

(sigNAL)
сигнал
horn

(RUL')
руль
steering wheel

(piDAL') *(tsiPLYEniya)*
педаль сцепления
clutch pedal

(piDAL') *(TORmaza)*
педаль тормоза
brake pedal

(SCHYOTka)
щётка
windshield wiper

(paNYEL') *(priBOrav)*
панель приборов
instrument panel (dashboard)

(ryCHAK) *(piriklyuCHYEniya)* *(skaraSTYEY)*
рычаг переключения скоростей
gear shift stick

(aksiliRATar) *(gas)*
акселератор (газ)
accelerator

(vitraVOye) *(stiKLO)*
ветровое стекло
windshield

(DVIgatil')
двигатель
motor

(radiAtar)
радиатор
radiator

(kaPOT)
капот
hood

(akumuLYAtar)
аккумулятор
battery

(faRY)
фары
headlights

(SVYET) (ZADniva) (KHOda)
свет заднего хода
backup light

(baGAZHnik)
багажник
trunk

(ZADniyi) (stiKLO)
заднее стекло
rear window

(ukaZAtil') *(pavaROta)*
указатель поворота
turn signal

(ZADni) *(faNAR')*
задний фонарь
rear light

(STOP-sigNAL)
стоп-сигнал
brakelight

(NOmir) *(maSHYny)*
номер машины
license plate

(binzakaLONka)
бензоколонка
gas pump

(akNO)
окно
window

(DVYERtsa)
дверца
door

(KRYsha)
крыша
roof

(shaSI)
шасси
body (of car)

(riSHOTka)
решётка
fender

(BAMpir)
бампер
bumper

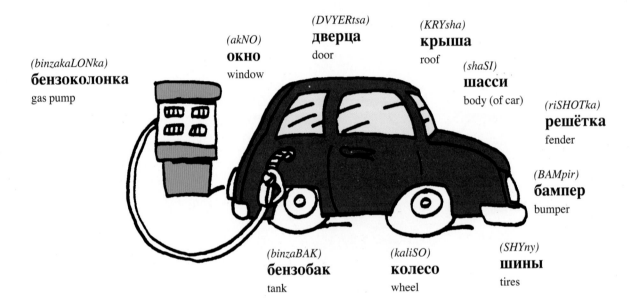

(binzaBAK)
бензобак
tank

(kaliSO)
колесо
wheel

(SHYny)
шины
tires

Now fill in the names of the following auto parts.

_____

_____

_____

_____

_____

_____

Помогите!

Help!

Here are some useful phrases in case of problems:

(spuSTIlas') *(SHYna)*
У меня спустилась шина.

I have a flat tire.

(zaVOditsa)
Машина не заводится.

The car doesn't start.

Она не идёт.

It doesn't go.

(pirigriVAitsa)
Она перегревается.

It overheats.

(KONchilsya)
Бензин кончился.

There's no more gas.

(radiAtar) *(pratiKAit)*
Радиатор протекает.

The radiator is leaking.

(akumuLYAtar) *(SYEL)*
Аккумулятор сел.

The battery is dead.

Проверьте, пожалуйста,

Please check the

　аккумулятор.

　　battery.

(tarmaZA)
　тормоза.

　　brakes.

(gluSHYtil')
　глушитель.

　　muffler.

　масло.

　　oil.

　шины.

　　tires.

Повелительное наклонение

Imperative mood

Do you want to say: "Read!" "Think!" "Go!" If you want other people to do something, you will have to use the verb in the "command" or "imperative" way. You have already seen and used several of these imperative forms, and they are easily recognized. In the chart below, note that there is a form for the familiar and singular, and a second form for the formal, polite, or plural.

To form the imperative from Russian verbs you must know the form for the third person plural (the "they" form). First remove the ending **ут/ют** or **ат/ят**.

If you are left with a vowel, add **й** for the familiar-singular and **йте** for the formal or plural.

(chiTAyut)	*(chiTAY)*	*(chiTAYtye)*
читают → чита +	**читай**	**читайте**
they read		

(DUmayut)	*(DUmay)*	*(DUmaytye)*
думают → дума +	**думай**	**думайте**
they think		

If you are left with two or more consonants after you drop the ending, add **и, ите**.

(POMnyat)	*(POMni)*	*(POMnitye)*
помнят → помн +	**помни**	**помните**
they remember		

If you are left with a singular consonant you must determine if the stress or accent can fall on the ending. (Hint: Is the ending in the "I" form stressed?) If the ending can be stressed, add **и, ите**.

(iDUT)	*(iDI)*	*(iDItye)*
идут → ид +	**иди**	**идите**
they go		

(gavaRYAT)	*(gavaRI)*	*(gavaRItye)*
говорят → говор +	**говори**	**говорите**
they speak/say		

If there is a single consonant, and the ending is never stressed, form the imperative by adding **ь, ьте**.

(gaTOvyat)	*(gaTOF')*	*(gaTOF'tye)*
готовят → готов +	**готовь**	**готовьте**
they prepare		

In the blanks below fill in the correct form of the formal imperative. (We have supplied the "they" form in parentheses).

1. Help me!   (помогут) _____ мне!

2. Check the oil.   (проверят) _____ масло.

3. Look here.   (смотрят) _____ сюда.

4. Go away!   (идут) _____ вон!

5. Don't forget!   (забудут)   Не _____ !

Осторожно! (Be careful!) Driving in a foreign country means watching the road even when the sights and sounds are so fascinating. **Очень красиво!** Yes, it's very beautiful! Read the following passage and learn the phrases that might come in useful some day. At the end of the passage you will be asked to answer a few questions. So pay close attention.

ПЕРВЫЙ ВОДИТЕЛЬ (First Driver)	*(BOzhi)* *(astaROZHna)* **Боже мой! Осторожно.**	My goodness! Be careful.
	(uMYEitye) **Вы умеете читать?**	Do you know how to read?
	(VIditye) **Вы не видите, что**	Can't you see that
	(PRAva) *(MNOY)* **право за мной?**	I have the right of way?
ВТОРАЯ ВОДИТЕЛЬНИЦА (Second Driver)	**Я знаю. Но вы едете**	I know. But you're driving
	150 км в час,	150 km per hour,
	(agraniCHEniye) **где 60 км ограничение.**	where the speed limit is 60.
ТРЕТЬЯ ВОДИТЕЛЬНИЦА (Third Driver)	*(paMOCH)* **Могу я вам помочь?**	May I help you?
ПЕРВЫЙ ВОДИТЕЛЬ	*(pazaVItye)* *(militsiaNYEra)* **Да. Позовите милиционера** *(pasmaTRYET')* *(sluCHIlas')* **посмотреть что случилось.**	Yes. Call the policeman to see what happened.

МИЛИЦИОНЕР (Policeman)	*(praisKHOdit)* **Что происходит?**	What's going on?
ПЕРВЫЙ ВОДИТЕЛЬ	*(stalkNUlis')* **Наши машины столкнулись.**	Our cars collided.
	(vinaVAta) **Она виновата.**	She's to blame.
ВТОРАЯ ВОДИТЕЛЬНИЦА	**Это не правда.**	That's not true.
	(sumaSHETshi) **Он водит как сумасшедший.**	He drives like a madman.
	(privySHAL) **И он превышал скорость.**	And he exceeded the speed limit.
МИЛИЦИОНЕР	*(niKTO)* *(RAnin)* **Никто не ранен? Хорошо.**	No one is injured? Good.
	(dakuMYENty) **Ваши документы, водительские права.**	Your documents, driver's licenses.
ВТОРАЯ ВОДИТЕЛЬНИЦА	*(paBLIzasti)* **Поблизости есть автосервис?**	Is there a repair shop nearby?
МИЛИЦИОНЕР	*(nidaliKO)* **Да. Недалеко по этой дороге. Два или три километра.**	Yes. Not far along this road. Two or three kilometers.

(В автосервисе)
(at the repair shop)

ВТОРАЯ ВОДИТЕЛЬНИЦА	*(pachiNIT')* **Вы можете машину починить?**	Can you repair the car?
МЕХАНИК (Mechanic)	*(pavizLO)* **Вам повезло. Нужно** *(smiNIT')* **будет сменить только бампер и фару.**	You're lucky. It will only be necessary to replace the bumper and a headlight.
ВТОРАЯ ВОДИТЕЛЬНИЦА	*(gaTOva)* **Когда машина будет готова?**	When will the car be ready?
МЕХАНИК	*(zapCHASti)* **У меня есть запчасти.**	I have the spare parts.
	(naVYERna) **Наверно, завтра днём.**	Probably tomorrow afternoon.

Try writing out the following phrases from the dialogue. They may come in handy.

1. May I help you? _____

2. Is there a repair shop nearby? _____

3. Can you repair a car? _____

4. When will the car be ready? _____

(YA) (khaCHU)   (YA) (maGU)   (YA) (BUdu)

Я хочу, я могу, я буду
I want   I can   I will

These three little verbs can be of great assistance to you. Try to learn them by heart!

ХОТЕТЬ	МОЧЬ	БЫТЬ
want	can	will
я хочу́	я могу́	я бу́ду
ты хо́чешь	ты мо́жешь	ты бу́дешь
она хо́чет	она мо́жет	она бу́дет
мы хоти́м	мы мо́жем	мы бу́дем
вы хоти́те	вы мо́жете	вы бу́дете
они хотя́т	они мо́гут	они бу́дут

Now fill in the blanks with the new verbs.

1. _____ поехать в Москву?
   Do you want to go to Moscow?

2. _____ водить машину?
   Does he want to drive the car?

3. _____ пойти в Кремль.
   I can't go to the Kremlin.

4. Когда оно _____ готово?
   When will it be ready?

5. Кто _____ мне помочь?
   Who can help me?

6. _____ во Владимире.
   They will be in Vladimir.

(FSYO) *(SHTO)* *(NAM)* *(NUZHna)*
ВСЁ ЧТО НАМ НУЖНО
Everything that we need

(paLATka)
палатка
tent

(aDYEZHda)
одежда
clothes

(DYEriva)
дерево
tree

(SONtse)
солнце
sun

(SPAL'ny) *(miSHOK)*
спальный мешок
sleeping bag

(karMAny) *(faNAR')*
карманный фонарь
flashlight

(midVYET')
медведь
bear

(bayDARka)
байдарка
canoe

(adiYAla)
одеяло
blanket

(tuaLYETnaya) *(buMAga)*
туалетная бумага
toilet paper

(karZINka)
корзинка
basket

(BANki)
банки
cans

(sapaGI)
сапоги
boots

(Udachka)
удочка
fishing rod

(SHTOpar)
штопор
corkscrew

(kaSTRYUli)
кастрюли
pots

(viDRO)
ведро
bucket

(tuaLYETny) *(priBOR)*
туалетный прибор
toilet kit

(RAdio)
радио
radio

(SPICHki)
спички
matches

That's a lot of new words and expressions to remember! Let's play a little game. Look at the word maze below and see how many words associated with camping you can identify. Circle the words and then write them out in the spaces below. We have already found the first word for you.

а	б	в	г	д	у	е	ё	р	а	д	и	о	с	я
ф	ш	т	в	е	д	р	о	м	б	п	ю	п	ь	ю
я	т	ш	я	ш	о	е	д	т	а	у	и	а	ы	т
ю	щ	т	а	с	ч	ф	е	ч	н	ч	ц	л	х	б
з	ж	о	ь	к	к	ь	я	л	к	м	н	а	н	х
щ	ю	п	ц	б	а	н	л	и	и	и	ы	т	ъ	д
л	о	о	у	ы	р	с	о	в	б	н	м	к	ъ	п
ь	ю	р	щ	к	а	с	т	р	ю	л	и	а	ц	б
т	у	а	л	е	т	н	ы	й	п	р	и	б	о	р

_____   _____
_____   _____
_____   _____
_____   _____

(KYEMpink)
КЕМПИНГ
Camping

Russians love to spend time in the country. As travel restrictions on foreigners have been relaxed in the past few years, camping has become an even easier and a more attractive option to see the vast expanses of Russia.

Mark and Caroline have already rented a car and are about to set off on their own. Let's see how they make out.

ANSWERS

Puzzle банки, ведро, кастрюли, одеяло, палатка, радио, спички, туалетный прибор, удочка, штопор

81

MARK	**Вы не скажете, где**	Could you tell me, where's
	(bliZHAYshi)	
	ближайший кемпинг?	the nearest campground?
ДЕВУШКА (Young Woman)	**Почти 20 километров**	About twenty kilometers
	(atSYUda)	
	отсюда. Там будет	from here. There will be
	(ZNAK) (palATkay)	
	знак с палаткой	a sign with a tent
	(siriDInye)	
	в середине.	in the middle.
MARK	**Вы не знаете, там можно**	Do you know if you can
	(DUSH)	
	принимать душ?	take a shower there?
ДЕВУШКА	*(paNYAtiya) (iMYEyu)*	
	Понятия не имею!	I don't have the slightest idea.
	(spraSItye) (MYEStye)	
	Спросите на месте.	Ask when you're there.

(pradaVOL'STvinam) *(magaZInye)*
В ПРОДОВОЛЬСТВЕННОМ МАГАЗИНЕ

In the grocery store

MARK	**Доброе утро. Мне нужно**	Good morning. I need
	(polkiLO) (SYra) (GRAM)	
	полкило сыра, 300 грамм	a half kilo of cheese, 300
	(vichiNY)	
	ветчины, и дайте	grams of ham, and give me
	(baTON) (KHLYEba)	
	батон хлеба.	a loaf of bread.
ХОЗЯЙКА	*(SHTO-nibut')* *(viNO)*	
	Ёще что-нибудь? Вино,	Anything else? Wine,
	(limaNAT) (YAblaki)	
	лимонад. Яблоки	soft drink? The apples are
	(FKUSny)	
	очень вкусны.	very tasty.

MARK	Спасибо. Это всё.	Thank you. That's all.
	Сколько с меня?	How much do I owe you?
ХОЗЯЙКА	Триста рублей.	Three hundred rubles.
MARK	Пожалуйста.	Here you are.
	До свидания.	Goodbye.

(MOZHna)   *(NUZHna)*   *(nil'ZYA)*

Можно, нужно, нельзя
It's possible,   it's necessary,   it's prohibited

Three more little words that can get you far. If you are asking for someone's permission or simply asking if it's possible, use **можно**.

If you need to do something or need a particular item, use **нужно**.

Please respect the sensitivities of your hosts. Remember that you are always a guest in a foreign country. If you hear **нельзя**, don't do it!

Let's see how successful you would be in locating a camping place and getting provisions for the night.

1. **Вы не скажете, где** _____ ?
   nearest campground

2. **Вы не знаете,** _____ ?
   can you take a shower there

3. _____ **полкило сыра.**
   I need

4. **Ёще что-нибудь?** _____ ?
   Wine, soft drink?

5. _____ ?
   How much do I owe you?

ANSWERS

Camping 1. ближайший кемпинг 2. там можно принимать душ 3. Мне нужно 4. Вино, лимонад? 5. Сколько с меня?

10

(vrimiNA)   *(GOda)*   *(MYEsitsy)*

Времена года, Месяцы
Seasons of the Year   Months

(paGOda)   *(DNI)*   *(niDYEli)*

Погода, Дни недели
Weather   Days of the Week

(ziMA)
ЗИМА
winter

январь

февраль

март

(viSNA)
ВЕСНА
spring

апрель

май

июнь

(LYEta)
ЛЕТО
summer

июль

август

сентябрь

(Osin')
ОСЕНЬ
fall

октябрь

ноябрь

декабрь

Месяцы

The months

(yinVAR')
январь
January

(aPRYEL')
апрель
April

(iYUL')
июль
July

(akTYABR')
октябрь
October

(fiVRAL')
февраль
February

(MAY)
май
May

(AVgust)
август
August

(naYABR')
ноябрь
November

(MART)
март
March

(iYUN')
июнь
June

(sinTYABR')
сентябрь
September

(diKABR')
декабрь
December

Погода

The weather

Какая сегодня погода?

How is the weather today?

Сегодня погода _____ .

The weather today is _____ .

(khaROshaya)
хорошая
good

(plaKHAya)
плохая
bad

Какая прекрасная погода!

What splendid weather!

Сегодня _____ .

Today it's _____ .

(tiPLO)
тепло
warm

(ZHARka)
жарко
hot

(praKHLADna)
прохладно
cool

(KHOladna)
холодно
cold

(SVYEtit) *(SONtse)*
Светит солнце.
The sun is shining.

(DUyit) *(VYEtir)*
Дует ветер.
The wind is blowing.

(iDYOT) *(DOSH)*
Идёт дождь.
It's raining.

(iDYOT) *(SNYEK)*
Идёт снег.
It's snowing.

Can you describe the weather in the pictures below?

1. _____   3. _____

2. _____   4. _____

Сегодня

		Вторник, 26 мая				Среда, 27 мая				Четверг, 28 мая			
		Ночь	Утро	День	Вечер	Ночь	Утро	День	Вечер	Ночь	Утро	День	Вечер
Температура,° С		+14..+18	+17..+19	+18..+12	+11..+13	+12..+19	+19..+16	+16..+13	+13..+12	+13..+19	+19..+16	+16..+13	+13..+12
Облачность и осадки													
Давление воздуха, mmHg		744	744	746	746	746	745	747	747	746	746	747	746
Направление и скорость ветра, мс		3	2	1	1	6	5	4	2	6	6	4	5
Долгота дня				0 07:39-21:40				4 08:51-21:41				8 10:10-21:42	
Фазы луны				●				●				●	

There are dozens of ways to find out the weather for your travels. Why not learn how to decipher the information in Russian language weather reports. Look at the chart above available on the internet at www.webmeteo.ru   You should easily recognize the days of the week and the date with day and month. Next you have the Russian words that you already know for night—**ночь**, morning—**утро**, day (afternoon)—**день** and evening—**вечер**. On the side you will note.

Температура	Temperature
Давление воздуха	Air pressure
Направление и скорость ветра	Wind direction and speed
Долгота дня	Length of the day
Фазы луны	Phases of the moon

Temperatures are given in degrees Celsius.

Temperature conversions

To change degrees Fahrenheit to Celsius subtract 32 and multiply by ⅝.

$$41°F - 32 = 9 \text{ x } \tfrac{5}{9} = 5°C$$

To convert from Celsius to Fahrenheit, multiply by ⅗ and add 32:

$$10°C \times \tfrac{9}{5} = 18 + 32 = 50°F$$

A quick method to get an approximate temperature is to take the degrees Fahrenheit, subtract 30 and divide by 2. From Celsius, multiply by 2 and add 30.

Most seasoned travelers know a few temperatures for reference.

ГРАДУСЫ
DEGREES

по Фаренгейту Fahrenheit		по Цельсию Celsius
212		100
98.6		37
86		30
77		25
68		20
50		10
32		0
14		–10
–04		–20
–22		–30
–40		–40

Термометр
Thermometer

It should be small consolation that at minus 40, degrees Fahrenheit and Celsius are identical.

(MNYE) (KHOladna)
Мне холодно.
It is cold to me.

(MNYE) (tiPLO)
Мне тепло.
It is warm to me.

When Russians say "I am cold, she is warm," etc., they are actually saying, "It is cold to me, to her, to him," etc. The person "to whom" or "for whom" something is done is placed in the **dative case**. This construction can help us express many feelings, so it's important to learn it. Look at the examples below. Note that the **dative case** form of the pronoun is placed before the word describing the action or state.

Мне жарко.
I'm hot.

Нам интересно.
We are interested.

Тебе холодно?
Are you cold?

Вам скучно?
Are you bored?

Ей/Ему плохо.
She's/He's not (feeling) well.

Им легко.
They have it easy.

Имена прилагательные

(imiNA) *(prilaGAtil'niye)*

Имена прилагательные

Adjectives

You have already noticed that Russian nouns can be masculine, feminine, and neuter, singular and plural. The adjectives and modifiers in Russian change their forms according to the noun they modify. You will need to know four basic forms of these words.

Masculine singular modifiers end most often in **ый**:
интересный, холодный
interesting   cold

If the ending is stressed, they end in **ой**:
большой
large

After **к, г, х, ш, щ, ч**, and **ж**, they end in **ий**:
русский, американский
Russian   American

Modifiers of feminine singular nouns end in **ая**:
интересная, большая, русская

Modifiers of neuter singular nouns end most often in **ое**:
интересное, холодное

After **ш, щ, ч, ц** and **ж**, if the ending is *not* stressed, they end in **ее**:
хорошее

Modifiers of most plural nouns end in **ые**:
интересные, холодные

After **к, г, х, ш, щ, ч**, and **ж**, they end in **ие**:
большие, русские, американские

Look at the pictures below and note how the adjectives combine with the nouns to form a phrase. For practice try writing the correct forms under the words.

Это

старый   человек.

_____   _____

молодая   девушка.

_____   _____

89

большое   зеркало.

_____   _____

маленькая   комната.

_____   _____

хорошая   гостиница.

_____   _____

высокая   девушка.

_____   _____

не высокая   девушка.

_____   _____

интересные   люди.

_____   _____

(aeraPORT)
Аэропорт
Airport

When you find the following useful words in the picture, write them out in the spaces provided.

(rigiSTRAtsiya) *(biLYEtaf)*
регистрация билетов _____
check in (registration)

(aviakamPAniya)
авиакомпания _____
airline

(baGASH)
багаж _____
luggage

(chiSY)
часы _____
clock

(PASpartny) *(kanTROL')*
паспортный контроль _____
passport control

(taMOZHnya)
таможня _____
customs

(LYOchik)
лётчик _____
pilot

(styuarDYEsa)
стюардесса _____
stewardess

(eskaLAtar)
эскалатор _____
escalator

(VYkhat)
выход _____
exit

(samaLYOT)

Самолёт

Airplane

Pronounce aloud the following items connected with airline flight as you search for some of them in the picture above. If you wish, you can write them out for practice.

(MYESta)
место
seat

_____

(saLON)
салон
cabin

_____

(riMYEN')
ремень
seat belt

_____

(pasaZHYR)
пасссажир
passenger

_____

(paSATka)
посадка
boarding

_____

(kaBIna)   (piLOta)
кабина пилота
cockpit

_____

(RYAT)
ряд
row

_____

(ekiPASH)
экипаж
crew

_____

(zapaSNOY)   (VYkhat)
запасной выход
emergency exit

_____

(VYlit)
вылет
takeoff

_____

(RYEYS)
рейс
flight

_____

(padNOS)
поднос
tray

_____

(LYOTnaye) (POlye)
лётное поле
runway

(NYE) (kuRIT')
НЕ КУРИТЬ
NO SMOKING

ТЕРМИНАЛ	СТАТУС	РЕЙС	НАПРАВЛЕНИЕ	ВРЕМЯ ПО РАСП.		СОСТОЯНИЕ
Терминал 1	SU	839	Санкт-Петербург	08:15		
Терминал 1	SU	733	Екатеринбург	08:20		
Терминал 1	D9	815	Омск	08:25		Отменен
Терминал 1	SU	785	Мин. Воды	08:35		
Терминал 1	SN	813	Самара	08:50		
Терминал 1	SU	869	Сочи	09:15		
Терминал 2	SU	295	Афины	09:20	Вылетел 16.12.08	09:33
Терминал 2	SU	237	Ларнака	09:35	Вылетел 16.12.08	09:39
Терминал 2	SU	293	Венеция	09:40	Вылетел 16.12.08	10:00
Терминал 2	SU	171	София	09:45	Вылетел 16.12.08	10:07
Терминал 2	SU	131	Будапешт	09:50	Вылетел 16.12.08	10:02
Терминал 2	SU	271	Женева	10:00	Вылетел 16.12.08	10:15
Терминал 2	SU	521	Дубай	10:00	Вылетел 16.12.08	10:25
Терминал 2	SU	229	Амстердам	10:10	Вылетел 16.12.08	10:20
Терминал 2	SU	101	Варшава	10:15	Вылетел 16.12.08	10:22
Терминал 2	SU	273	Ницца	10:20	Вылетел 16.12.08	10:27
Терминал 2	SU	125	Гамбург	10:25	Вылетел 16.12.08	10:31
Терминал 2	SU	259	Париж	10:30	Вылетел 16.12.08	10:50
Терминал 2	SU	121	Мюнхен	10:40	Вылетел 16.12.08	13:53

Notice that the flight to Omsk has been cancelled—**Отменен**. Some others have already departed—**Вылетел**. Can you identify some of the international destinations, like Athens, Venice, Dubai, Paris? Try reading the names aloud. While not identical to their English counterparts, many names of cities are close enough in most cases to be recognized.

Mark and his family are on their way back to Moscow and have decided to fly instead of taking the train.

ALEX	*(miSTA)* **Папа, где наши места?**	Papa, where are our seats?
СТЮАРДЕССА (Stewardess)	*(paSAdochny)* *(taLON)* **Ваш посадочный талон.**	Your boarding pass.
MARK	**Вы можете**	Can you
	нам помочь? Мы все	help us? We are all
	(uSTAli) **устали.**	tired.
СТЮАРДЕССА	**С удовольствием.**	With pleasure.
	(RYAT) **Ряд 21, места А, Б, В, Г.**	Row 21, Seats A, B, V, G.
ALEX	*(BUditye)* *(karMIT')* **Вы будете нас кормить?**	Will you be feeding us?
СТЮАРДЕССА	*(priniSU)* **Я вам принесу обед**	I will bring you dinner
	после вылета.	after takeoff.
ПИЛОТ (Pilot)	*(priVYETSTvuyim)* **Приветствуем вас на**	We welcome you on
	(barTU) *(paLYOT)* **борту. Наш полёт в**	board. Our flight to
	Москву длится 3 часа.	Moscow takes 3 hours.
	(vysaTA) **Высота полёта 10,000**	Our altitude is 10,000
	метров. Скорость	meters. The speed is
	750 км. в час.	750 km per hour.
СТЮАРДЕССА	*(PROsim)* *(pristigNUT')* **Просим вас пристегнуть**	We request you to fasten
	(rimNI) *(kuRIT')* **ремни.**	seat belts.
MARK	**Нина, пристегни ремень.**	Nina, fasten your belt.
	(vyliTAyim) **Мы вылетаем.**	We are taking off.

СТЮАРДЕССА	Дорогие пассажиры,	Dear passengers,
	через несколько минут	in a few minutes
	(prizimLIMsya)	
	мы приземлимся в	we will be landing in
	Москве. Температура	Moscow. The temperature
	плюс 5 градусов. Идет	is plus five degrees. It's
	дождь.	raining.

	(KHOchitsa)	
ALEX	Девушка, мне хочется	Miss, I would like
	(paPIT')	
	чего-нибудь попить.	something to drink.
СТЮАРДЕССА	*(k) (sazhaLYEniyu)*	
	К сожалению, уже	Unfortunately, it's already
	поздно. Я сейчас вам	late. In just a minute
	(kanFYETku)	
	принесу конфетку.	I'll bring you a piece of candy.
MARK	Смотри, Нина. Мы уже	Look, Nina. We're already
	(ZDYES')	
	здесь.	here.

Try matching the important phrases in column one with those in column two. Write out the Russian for practice.

1. **Вы можете нам помочь?**   **а.** We are all tired.

_____

2. **Мы все устали.**   **б.** No Smoking.

_____

3. **Не курить.**   **в.** Can you help us?

_____

4. Мы приземлимся в Москве.

г. I would like something to drink.

_____

5. Мне хочется чего-нибудь попить.

д. We will be landing in Moscow.

_____

Будущее время
Future time

You may have already noticed that Russians have two ways to form the **future tense**, that we in English form with the help of the words "will" or "shall."

Just as in English, Russians can form a **compound future** consisting of two words. The first component is a form of the verb "to be."

я бу́ду	I will be
ты бу́дешь	you will be
он/она/оно бу́дет	he/she/it will be
мы бу́дем	we will be
вы бу́дете	you will be
они бу́дут	they will be

You can form the **future tense** of most verbs we have seen by combining the infinitive of these **imperfective verbs** with the proper form of бу́ду.

I will listen.	Я бу́ду слу́шать.
You will read.	Ты бу́дешь чита́ть.
It will cost.	Оно бу́дет стои́ть.
We will hurry.	Мы бу́дем спеши́ть.
You will speak Russian.	Вы бу́дете говори́ть по-ру́сски.
They will feed us.	Они нас бу́дут корми́ть.

Russians can also form a **simple future** from a **"perfective"** verb. In this instance, you already know all of the forms of the verbs because they are identical to those of the **present tense**. Look at the following example.

Present		Future	
I read	я читáю	I will read	я почитáю
you speak	ты говорúшь	you will speak	ты поговорúшь
she is hurrying	она спешúт	she will hurry	она поспешúт

The examples show us one way in which a **perfective verb** can be formed from an **imperfective verb** by adding a prefix. The prefix **по** often means "just a little." Russians simply know which verbs are **imperfective** and **perfective**. For the moment, just concentrate on the meanings of verbs when you encounter them in our dialogues. We'll give you an easy way to check on the aspect of verbs at the end of the book in the Russian-English dictionary.

(FSYO)   *(FSYE)*

Всё — Все

Everything — Everyone

In only a few word pairs is the difference between the letters **ё** and **e** as important as in **всё** meaning "everything" and **все** meaning "all the people" or "everyone."

Watch how they are used.

Всё в порядке.	Everything (all) is in order.
Все идут домой.	Everyone is (all are) going home.

Remember: in Russian **все** takes a plural verb, but in English "everyone" takes a singular verb. Since Russians normally do not print or write the two dots on the letter **ё**, you will have to rely on the context to understand if they mean **всё** or **все**. Watch how they are used in the next dialogue.

(ekSKURsiya) *(pa)* *(krimLYU)*
Экскурсия по Кремлю

An excursion around the Kremlin

Caroline, Stephanie, and Alex have decided to take a tour of the Kremlin this afternoon.

ЭКСКУРСОВОД (Tour Guide)	*(naKHOdimsya)* **Мы теперь находимся на территории Московского Кремля.**	We are now located on the territory of the Moscow Kremlin.
CAROLINE	**Скажите, пожалуйста, где** *(arKHANgilski)* *(saBOR)* **Архангельский собор.**	Please tell us where The Cathedral of the Archangel is.
ЭКСКУРСОВОД	*(tuDA)* **Мы туда идем.** *(pakaZHU)* **Я вам покажу.**	We are going there. I'll show you.
ALEX	*(pakhaROniny)* **Там похоронены бывшие** *(tsaRI)* **цари.**	The former tsars are buried there.

ЭКСКУРСОВОД	*(druGIye)* **Вы видели другие** **достопримечательности?**	Have you seen the other sights?
STEPHANIE	**Я хочу посмотреть** *(TSAR'-KOlakal)* **Царь-колокол и** *(TSAR'-PUSHku)* **Царь-пушку.**	I want to look at the Tsar Bell and the Tsar Cannon.
ЭКСКУРСОВОД	**Конечно. Все хотят** **их посмотреть.**	Of course. Everyone wants to see them.
CAROLINE	*(dalzhNY)* **Мы должны спешить.** **На два часа у нас билеты** *(aruZHEYnuyu)* *(paLAtu)* **в Оружейную палату.**	We have to hurry. At two o'clock we have tickets to the Armory.
ЭКСКУРСОВОД	*(zaBUtye)* **Не забудьте посмотреть** *(KRASnuyu)* *(PLOschat')* **Красную площадь и** **смену караула.**	Don't forget to see Red Square and the changing of the guard.
ALEX	*(intiRYESna)* **Всё так интересно.**	Everything is so interesting.

ENTERTAINMENT

(razvliCHEniye)
Развлечение

	(tiATR)	*(kiNO)*	*(PRAZniki)*
12	**Театр,**	**Кино,**	**Праздники**
	Theater	Movies	Holidays

(tiATR)
ТЕАТР
Theater

Boris and Alexandra, a middle-aged couple from Omaha, Nebraska, are making their first visit to Russia. They both enjoy the theater. They are in Moscow on the second day of their stay. Being of Russian descent, they both speak some Russian. "Not one word of English during our vacation," they decide.

БОРИС	*(payTI)* **Ты хочешь пойти в театр сегодня вечером?**	Do you want to go to the theater this evening?
АЛЕКСАНДРА	*(zamiCHAtil'naya)* **Замечательная идея!**	A wonderful idea!
БОРИС	**В Большом театре балет «Лебединое озеро». Во Дворце съездов опера «Борис Годунов».**	In the Bolshoi Theater there's the ballet *Swan Lake*. In the Palace of Congresses there's the opera *Boris Godunov*.
АЛЕКСАНДРА	*(Opiru)* **Я люблю оперу, но** *(SLISHkam)* **четыре часа слишком долго.**	I love opera, but four hours is too long.
БОРИС	*(saGLAsin)* *(ravNO)* **Я согласен. Всё равно,** *(baLYET)* **я предпочитаю балет.**	I agree. All the same, I prefer the ballet.
АЛЕКСАНДРА	**Позвони в театральную** *(vniZU)* **кассу. Она внизу.**	Call the theater ticket desk. It's downstairs.

100

БОРИС	*(biLYEty)* **Если есть билеты,**	If there are tickets available,
	(balKOnye) **я закажу два на балконе.**	I'll order two in the balcony.
АЛЕКСАНДРА	**Пока. Я пойду в**	See you later. I'm going to
	(SAUnu) **сауну.**	the sauna.

Many Russian and English words are similar. Always try to pronounce the Russian word aloud and you'll be pleasantly surprised with how many you can recognize. To help you remember them write out the words you will want to have «**на кончике языка**» ("on the tip of the tongue").

(tiAtr)
театр   theater

_____

(balKON)
балкон   balcony

_____

(kaMYEdiya)
комедия   comedy

_____

(traGYEdiya)
трагедия   tragedy

_____

(iDYEya)
идея   idea

_____

(baLYET)
балет   ballet

_____

(Opira)
опера

opera

(miLOdiya)
мелодия

melody

(kiNO)

КИНО

Movies

Boris and Alexandra are discussing what movie they want to see.

АЛЕКСАНДРА	**Пойдем в кино!**	Let's go to the movies.
БОРИС	*(nidaliKO)* **В кинотеатре недалеко**	In the movie theater not
	(savriMYEny) **идёт современный**	far away a contemporary
	русский фильм.	Russian film is playing.
АЛЕКСАНДРА	*(TItrami)* **Фильм с титрами?**	A film with subtitles?
БОРИС	**Нет, без титров.**	No. Without subtitles.
	Но ты будешь понимать	But you will be able to understand
	(pachTI) **почти всё.**	almost everything.

В кассе (At the ticket office)

АЛЕКСАНДРА	**Два билета на**	Two tickets to the
	(viCHYERni) *(siANS)* **вечерний сеанс.**	evening performance.
КАССИРША	*(paBLIzhe)* *(paDAL'she)* **Поближе или подальше?**	Closer or further away (from the screen)?

БОРИС	*(BLISka)* **Не слишком близко.**	Not too close.
	(zaBYL) *(achKI)* **Я забыл мои очки.**	I forgot my eyeglasses.
АЛЕКСАНДРА	*(raskaZHU)* **Ничего. Я тебе расскажу,** **кто что делает.**	Never mind. I'll tell you who is doing what.
БОРИС	**Я так рад, что мы** *(VMEStye)* **всё делаем вместе.**	I'm so glad that we do everything together.
АЛЕКСАНДРА	**И я так рада.**	I'm so glad too.

(mistaiMYEniye)   *(i)* *(imiNA)*   *(suschistVItil'niye)*

Местоимение и Имена Существительные

Pronouns and nouns

Direct objects

We have already seen and heard several pronouns used in the **dative cases**: **Мне холодно, Вам скучно**. When some action is performed on someone or something, a direct object is required. Even in English the pronouns have different forms in the **accusative case**; for example, "I see you," "he hears me." Look at the examples below of Russian nouns and pronouns in the **accusative case**, and pay special attention to the forms you will most frequently use.

ACCUSATIVE CASE

Nouns

Feminine nouns.   When the nominative case ends in **a**, the accusative case ends in **y**.

Эта книга.   **Она понимает книгу.**
This is a book.   She understands the book.

When the nominative case ends in **я**, the accusative case ends in **ю**.

Это моя тётя.   **Я люблю тётю.**
This is my aunt.   I love my aunt.

Neuter nouns have the same nominative and accusative case endings.

Где зеркало?   **Я вижу зеркало.**
Where is the mirror?   I see the mirror.

Continued on next page

Inanimate masculine nouns have identical nominative and accusative cases.

Это наш дом.
This is our house.

Я знаю ваш дом.
I know your house.

Animate (people and animals) masculine nouns end in **a** or **я** in the accusative case.

Это студент.
This is a student.
Это Евгений.
This is Yevgeny.

Она видит студента.
She sees the student.
Я знаю Евгения.
I know Yevgeny.

Pronouns

Nominative Case			Accusative Case	
I	я		me	меня
you	ты		you	тебя
she	она		her	её
he/it	он/оно		him/it	его
we	мы		us	нас
you	вы		you	вас
they	они		them	их

In many cases the object pronouns will come before the verb. Watch how they can be used to replace nouns.

I am reading a book.	**Я читаю книгу.**	I am reading it.	**Я её читаю.**
We love the theater.	**Мы любим театр.**	We love it.	**Мы его любим.**

Now try to replace the noun in italics with the proper form of the pronoun.

1. **Я понимаю этот *фильм*.** Я _____ понимаю.

2. **Я знаю эту *женщину*.** Я _____ знаю.

3. **Она любит *оперу*.** Она _____ любит.

4. **Они приносят *книги*.** Они _____ приносят.

ANSWERS

Fill in 1. его 2. её 3. её 4. их

104

Праздники

Holidays

1 января	*(NOvy) (GOT)* **Новый год**	January 1 — New Year's Day
7 января	*(razhdistVO) (khriSTOva)* **Рождество Христово**	January 7 — Orthodox Christmas
23 февраля	*(DYEN') (zaSCHITnika)* **День защитника** *(aTYEchistva)* **Отечества**	February 23 — Day of the Defender of the Fatherland
8 марта	*(mizhdunaRODny)* **Международный** *(ZHENski) (DYEN')* **женский день**	March 8 — International Women's Day
1 мая	*(PYERvaye) (MAya)* **Первое мая**	May 1 — May Day Workers' Day
9 мая	*(DYEN') (paBYEdy)* **День победы**	May 9 — Victory Day
12 июня	*(DYEN') (raSIyi)* **День России**	June 12 — Day of Russia
4 ноября	*(DYEN') (naRODnava) (yiDINstva)* **День народного единства**	November 4 — Day of National Unity

(z) (DNYOM) (razhDYEniya)
С днём   рождения!

Happy Birthday!

(S) (PRAZnikam)
С праздником!

Happy holiday!

(s) (NOvym)   (GOdam)
С Новым годом!

Happy New Year!

Russian Orthodox Churches still observe Christmas and Easter according to the old Julian calendar that was in use in Russia until the Gregorian calendar was adopted in 1918.

(s) (razhdistVOM)   (khriSTOvym)
С Рождеством Христовым!
(khriSTOS)   (vasKRYEsye)
Христос воскресе!

Merry Christmas! (With the Birth of Christ)

Happy Easter! (Christ Is Risen)

АЛЕКСАНДР	**Вася, какие у вас праздники?**	Vasya, which holidays do you have?
ВАСИЛИЙ	*(praSTOY)* *(vaPROS)* **Это не простой вопрос.** *(RAN'shi)* **Раньше были** *(kamuniSTIchiskiye)* **коммунистические** **праздники, как 7 ноября,** *(viLIkaya)* *(akTYABR'skaya)* **Великая Октябрьская** *(rivaLYUtsiya)* **Революция.**	That is not a simple question. Previously there were communist holidays like November 7, Revolution Day.
СТЕФАНИ	**А Новый год?**	And New Year's?
ВАСИЛИЙ	**Да, 1 января.** **8 марта, Международный** **женский день тоже** *(papuLYARny)* **популярный праздник.**	Yes, January 1. March 8, International Women's Day, is also a popular holiday
АЛЕКСАНДР	*(fstriCHAitye)* **А как вы встречаете** **Рождество?**	And how do you celebrate Christmas ?
ВАСИЛИЙ	**Мы встречаем Рождество** **7 января.** **Это 25 декабря** *(STAramu)* *(kalindaRYU)* **по старому календарю.**	We celebrate Christmas January 6. That is December 25 on the old calendar.
СТЕФАНИ	*(YOLka)* **А ёлка?**	And the tree?
ВАСИЛИЙ	**И ёлка есть, и** *(DYET)* *(maROS)* **Дед Мороз.**	There's a tree, and Father Frost [Russia's Santa Claus].

АЛЕКСАНДР	Я знаю, что вы все страдали во время войны.	I know that you all suffered during the time of the war.
ВАСИЛИЙ	Да. Каждый год мы помним День победы 9 мая.	Yes. Each year we remember Victory Day on May 9.
АЛЕКСАНДР	Я знаю ещё один день. 1 мая.	I know one more day. May Day, May 1.

Now see if you can connect the days on the left with the correct holidays.

1.	1 января	а.	День победы.
2.	7 января	б.	Новый год.
3.	8 марта	в.	Рождество.
4.	9 мая	г.	Октябрьская революция.
5.	7 ноября	д.	Международный женский день.

ANSWERS

Holidays 1. б 2. в 3. д 4. а 5. г

13 | *(SPORT)* СПОРТ

Sport(s)

(khaDIT) *(f)* *(paKHOdy)* *(i)* *(BYEgat')*
ХОДИТЬ В ПОХОДЫ И БЕГАТЬ

Going on hikes and jogging

Caroline Smith is in great shape. She jogs every morning. Sometimes she is joined by her husband and children, but they can barely keep up. This morning she is approached by a newspaper reporter who is writing an article on sports.

КОРРЕСПОНДЕНТ (Reporter)	*(gaspaZHA)* Доброе утро, госпожа. Я *(karispanDYENT)* корреспондент. Можно *(zaDAT')* вам задать несколько вопросов?	Good morning. Miss. I am a reporter. May I ask you a few questions?
CAROLINE	Пожалуйста. Только *(MYEDlina)* говорите медленно. Я американка и не понимаю всё.	Please. Only speak slowly. I am an American and do not understand everything.
КОРРЕСПОНДЕНТ	*(CHASta)* *(BYEgaitye)* Вы часто бегаете?	Do you jog often?
CAROLINE	Я бегаю каждое утро. *(inagDA)* Иногда мой муж и дети бегают со мной.	I run every morning. Sometimes my husband and children run with me.

КОРРЕСПОНДЕНТ	*(NOsit)* **Что люди носят в Америке, когда они бегают?**	What do people wear in America when they jog?
CAROLINE	*(aBYCHna)* **Обычно мы носим** *(sparTIVny)* **спортивный костюм и** *(kraSOFki)* **кроссовки.**	Usually we wear a jogging suit and sneakers.
КОРРЕСПОНДЕНТ	**Какие другие виды спорта вы любите?**	What other types of sport do you like?
CAROLINE	**Моя семья очень любит ходить в походы.**	My family really likes to go on hikes.
КОРРЕСПОНДЕНТ	**Ваш муж любит смотреть спорт по** *(tiliVIzaru)* **телевизору?**	Does your husband like to watch sports on television?
CAROLINE	**И как ещё! Он смотрит** *(fudBOL)* *(baskidBOL)* **футбол или баскетбол каждую субботу.**	And how! He watches soccer or basketball every Saturday.
КОРРЕСПОНДЕНТ	*(intirV'YU)* **Спасибо за интервью.**	Thank you for the interview.

(gaspaDIN)   *(gaspaZHA)*

господин, госпожа
   Mr.   Miss or Mrs.

   In the days of the Soviet Union, a general means of address was **товарищ** (comrade). Today Russians are likely to use the terms once reserved for foreigners: **господин** for Mr., **госпожа** for Miss or Mrs. And, of course, you might hear **Дамы и господа** (Ladies and Gentlemen).

   Another way to address someone is to say, **молодой человек** (young man) or **девушка** (Miss). Even for older people these expressions are a delightful compliment. Recently, Russians have begun using the term, **женщина** for Mrs. or any middle-aged woman.

КУПАТЬСЯ И ПЛАВАТЬ

(kuPAtsa) *(i)* *(PLAvat')*

Bathing and swimming

(kuPAitsa)
Марк купается.
bathes

(PLAvait)
Каролина плавает.
swims

(PLAFki)
Он носит плавки.
swim trunks

(kuPAL'nik)
Она носит купальник.
bathing suit

(brass)
брасс
breaststroke

(KROL)
кроль
crawl

(PLAvaniye) *(na)* *(spiNYE)*
плавание на спине
backstroke

Марк отдыхает.
is resting

Каролина загорает.
is sunbathing

Verbs with СЯ

Some Russian verbs have the particle **ся** or **сь** added after the required ending. Compare the conjugation of the verbs **плавать** (to swim) and **купаться** (to bathe).

плавать	купаться
я плаваю	я купаюсь
ты плаваешь	ты купаешься
она плавает	он купается
мы плаваем	мы купаемся
вы плаваете	вы купаетесь
они плавают	они купаются

Note that after consonants, including the soft sign **ь**, you add **ся**. After a vowel letter, you must add **сь**.

110

Now try your hand at adding the correct endings to some of the verbs below.

1. **Максим, где ты купа** _____ **?** (bathe, go swimming)

2. **Ирина и Сергей, вы всегда купа** _____ **утром.** (bathes, goes swimming)

3. **Наши дети никогда не слуша** _____ **.** (obey)

4. **Почему Марк улыба** _____ **.** (smiling)

5. **Я умыва** _____ **до завтрака.** (wash up)

Before we go out to do some exercise, let's try to answer a few simple questions.

а. **Что делает Каролина?** _____

б. **Что делает Марк?** _____

в. **Что это?** _____

г. **Что это?** _____

д. **Что это?** _____

ORDERING A MEAL
(zakaZAT)   *(aBYET)*
Заказать обед

In Russia you will certainly want to taste the fine local cuisine. Be sure you don't miss out on the **икра** (caviar) and **блины** (blinis), accompanied, of course, by **водка**. You'll also want to try the **пирожки** (meat or cabbage pies), **борщ** (borscht) and **чёрный хлеб** (black bread).

(MNYE)   *(NRAvitsa)*
Мне нравится . . .
I like it. . .

(YA) *(LYUblyu)*
Я люблю . . .
I love it. . .

You'll want to be able to distinguish between liking something or someone and loving it or her/him. When Russians say "I like it," they are actually saying, "It is pleasing to me." Note that the person or object liked will be the subject of the sentence in the **nominative case** — the form given in dictionaries and word lists. When Russians say, "I love him, her, it," they must use the direct object form in the **accusative case**.

Notice the difference in the following examples:

Мне нравится суп.   **Я люблю суп.**

Мне нравится молоко.   **Я люблю молоко.**

Мне нравится водка. **Я люблю водку.**

Notice that the feminine noun for vodka (**водка**) changes the
«**а**» to «**у**» in the **accusative case.**

Here are a few for you to try. Write in the answer for things you really love!

1. **Мне нравится чай.**  Я люблю _____.

2. **Мне нравится масло.** Я люблю _____.

3. **Мне нравится рыба.** Я люблю _____.

4. **Мне нравится мясо.**  Я люблю _____.

5. **Мне нравится сок.** Я люблю _____.

6. **Мне нравится курица.**  Я люблю _____.

ЗАВТРАК
(ZAFtrak)

Breakfast

(buFYET)

буфет

snack bar

БОРИС	**Что на завтрак?**		What's for breakfast?
АЛЕКСАНДРА	**Яблочный или**		Apple or
	(vinaGRADny) **виноградный сок.**		grape juice.

БОРИС (to server)	**Один кофе** *(malaKOM)* **с молоком.**		One coffee with milk.

ДЕВУШКА	*(SYR)* **Что ещё? Сыр?**		What else? Cheese?

АЛЕКСАНДРА	*(CHYORny)* *(KHLYEP)* **Да, и чёрный хлеб.**		Yes, and black bread.

БОРИС	*(MAsla)* **И масло** *(vaRYEn'ye)* **и варенье.**		And butter and jelly.

АЛЕКСАНДРА	*(CHASHku)* **Мне чашку чая** *(SAkharam)* **с сахаром.**		For me a cup of tea with sugar.

БОРИС	**Сколько с нас?**	How much do we owe?
ДЕВУШКА	**Сто рублей.**	One hundred rubles.

114

Fill in the blanks below and then repeat the sentences so that you will be able to order breakfast too.

1. Вам чёрный кофе или _____?

2. Вы предпочитаете варенье или _____?

3. Мне очень нравится _____ .

4. Мы все любим чёрный _____ .

(STOL)

СТОЛ

The table

(baKAL)	*(staKAN)*	*(CHASHka)*
бокал	**стакан**	**чашка**
wine glass	glass	cup

(SOL' i PYErits)
соль и перец
salt and pepper

(SAkhar)
сахар
sugar

(salFYETka)
салфетка
napkin

(NOSH)
нож
knife

(VILka)	*(LOSHka)*	*(taRYELka)*
вилка	**ложка**	**тарелка**
fork	spoon	plate

(aBYET)

ОБЕД

Lunch/Dinner

The main meal of the day for Russians is **обед**. It is likely to consist of appetizers or a salad, soup, a main course, and a light dessert. All of this is accompanied by plenty of bread, and perhaps a glass of wine, vodka or mineral water.

Look at the picture below and see if you can find the following items:

(zaKUSki)
закуски
appetizers

(SUP)
суп
soup

(viNO)
вино
wine

(Ovaschi)
овощи
vegetables

(RYba)
рыба
fish

(saLAT)
салат
salad

(FRUKty)
фрукты
fruits

(MYAsa)
мясо
meat

(YA) (vaz'MU)

Я возьму . . .

I'll take

ВЗЯТЬ	
Я возьму	мы возьмём
ты возьмёшь	вы возьмёте
он/она возьмёт	они возьмут

At the snack bar or in the restaurant you will be asked what you want to order. Use the forms of the verb **взять** (take) to tell your hostess what you and your family want.

1. **Моя жена возьм** _____ _____.

2. **Моя дочь возьм** _____  _____.

3. **Мой сын возьм** _____ _____.

4. **Я возьм** _____  _____.

5. **Мы все возьм** _____ _____.

(Uzhin)

УЖИН

Supper

If you have a full meal at midday, you will probably want only a light supper — **ужин.** This could be at a friend's house or at the theater buffet. One of the nicest buffet suppers is available before the performance at the Palace of Congresses (**Дворец съездов**).

Дайте мне, пожалуйста   Please, give me:

один бутерброд
one sandwich

два бутерброда
two sandwiches

три бутерброда
three sandwiches

четыре бутерброда
four sandwiches

(iKROY)
с икрой
with caviar

(SYram)
с сыром
with cheese

(vichiNOY)
с ветчиной
with ham

(kalbaSOY)
с колбасой
with salami

пять бутербродов
five sandwiches

шесть бутербродов
six sandwiches

(asiTRInay)
с осетриной
with sturgeon

(SYEMgay)
с сёмгой
with salmon

Что будем пить?   What shall we drink?

(staKAN)
один стакан

(shamPANskava)
шампанского

(buTYLku)
одну бутылку

(limaNAda)
лимонада

две   бутылки

(miniRAL'nay)   *(vaDY)*
минеральной воды

А на сладкое?   And for dessert?

(toRT)
торт
cake

(piROZHnaye)
пирожное
a pastry

(maROzhinaye)
мороженое
ice cream

(piCHYEn'ye)
печенье
cookie

Let's see if we can remember some of the more important words from our dining experiences.

1. What are the three meals of the day? _____ , _____ ,

_____ .

2. Write three things you would like for breakfast:

_____   _____   _____

3. Write down and pronounce aloud your choices for a full dinner.

_____   _____   _____

_____   _____   _____

_____   _____   _____

4. Can you order supper for your guest at the theater buffet? She would like a sandwich with caviar, a glass of champagne, some pastry and a cup of tea.

_____   _____

_____   _____

Now match the words or expressions in the column on the right with the item most closely associated with it on the left.

1.	чай	а.	ложка
2.	вилка	б.	соль
3.	хлеб	в.	с сахаром
4.	кофе	г.	с молоком
5.	перец	д.	белый и чёрный

The following word puzzle contains several choices for the dinner menu. See if you can find all six:

а	б	с	а	л	а	т	ж
в	д	у	з	х	в	ш	ю
ш	и	п	ж	ц	и	м	я
р	ы	б	а	щ	н	я	т
я	ш	е	щ	т	о	с	у
в	с	л	а	д	к	о	е

Ресторан / Чаевые

The Restaurant   Tips

(miNYU)   *(paZHAluysta)*

Меню, пожалуйста.

The menu, please.

At the restaurant, remember the expressions
for "bringing" and "taking":

(priniSItye)   *(paZHAluysta)*

Принесите, пожалуйста . . .   *Please bring . . .*

(YA) (siCHAS) (priniSU)

Я сейчас принесу.   *I'll bring it right away.*

(YA) (vaz'MU)

Я возьму . . .   *I'll take . . .*

МЕНЮ

(zaKUski) **закуски**	appetizers	*(saLAT)* **салат**	salad
(khaLODniye) **холодные**	cold	*(ftaROye)* **второе**	second (course)
(gaRYAchiye) **горячие**	hot	*(RYba)* **рыба**	fish
		(MYAsa) **мясо**	meat
		(PTItsa) **птица**	poultry
		(Ovaschi) **овощи**	vegetables
		(FRUKty) **фрукты**	fruits
(PYERvaye) **первое**	first (course)	*(TRYEt'e)* **третье**	third (course)
(SUP) **суп**	soup	*(SLATkaye)* **сладкое**	dessert (sweets)
		(naPITki) **напитки**	beverages

Caroline and Mark have decided to have dinner in a fine Russian restaurant. After they have
been seated and have studied the menu, the waiter approaches. They are ready to order.

ОФИЦИАНТ (Waiter)	**Добрый вечер. Я** *(SLUshayu)* **вас слушаю.**	Good evening. I'm at your service.
МАРК	**Что вы нам** *(pasaVYEtuitye)* **посоветуете?**	What can you recommend to us?
ОФИЦИАНТ	**Если вы любите** *(iKRU)* **икру, у нас и** *(CHORnay) (KRASnaya)* **чёрная и красная.**	If you like caviar, we have both black and red.
КАРОЛИНА	**Я возьму чёрную.**	I'll take the black.
МАРК	**А мне** *(asarTI) (misNOye)* **ассорти мясное.**	And for me the assorted meats.
ОФИЦИАНТ	*(saLAT)* **Кто хочет салат?**	Who would like salad?
МАРК	**Я возьму русский** **салат.**	I'll take the Russian salad.
ОФИЦИАНТ	**Вы будете суп?**	Will you be having soup?
КАРОЛИНА	*(paPRObavat)* **Я хочу попробовать** **русский борщ.**	I want to try the Russian borscht.
ОФИЦИАНТ	**А на второе?**	And for the main course?
МАРК	*(FIRminiye)* **Какие у вас фирменные** *(BLYUda)* **блюда?**	What are the house specialties?
ОФИЦИАНТ	*(rikaminDUyu)* **Я очень рекомендую** *(asiTRInu)* **осетрину.**	I highly recommend the sturgeon.
КАРОЛИНА	**Мне, пожалуйста,** *(laSOsya)* **лосося.**	For me, the salmon, please.
МАРК	*(tsyPLYONka)* **Я возьму цыплёнка.**	I'll take the chicken.
ОФИЦИАНТ	**Что вы будете** **пить?**	What will you be drinking?
КАРОЛИНА	**Красное вино, пожалуйста.**	Red wine, please.
МАРК	*(buTYLku)* **Принесите бутылку,** **и сто грамм водки.**	Bring a bottle, and 100 grams of vodka.

ОФИЦИАНТ	Кофе или чай?	Coffee or tea?
КАРОЛИНА	Чай с лимоном, и мороженое.	Tea with lemon, and ice cream.
МАРК	Дайте мне кофе и пирожное.	Give me some coffee and a pastry.
ОФИЦИАНТ	Это всё?	Is that all?
МАРК	Я думаю, что да.	I think so.
КАРОЛИНА	А! Чёрный хлеб и масло.	Ah! Black bread and butter.
ОФИЦИАНТ	Сейчас принесу.	I'll bring it right away.

(tuaLYEty)
Туалеты
Restrooms

After their meal, Mark and Caroline both want to freshen up.

(ZHENski)
женский
ladies'

(muSHKOY)
мужской
men's

Да или Нет?

Read back over the dialogue between the waiter and Caroline and Mark. Then examine the statements and fill in the blanks with **Да** or **Нет** (True or False).

1. **Каролина возьмёт чёрную икру.** _____

2. **Марк хочет попробовать русский борщ.** _____

3. **Официант рекомендует цыплёнка.** _____

4. **Марк и Каролина любят красное вино.** _____

5. **Каролина хочет белый хлеб.** _____

6. **Марк будет пить кофе.** _____

7. **Каролина возьмёт мороженое.** _____

122

It's finally time for Caroline and Mark to pay for their meal.

МАРК	Дайте нам, пожалуйста, счёт.	Please, give us the bill.
ОФИЦИАНТ	Пожалуйста.	Here it is.
МАРК	Всё было очень вкусно. Обслуживание входит в счёт?	Everything was delicious. Is service included in the bill?
ОФИЦИАНТ	Да. 10 процентов.	Yes. Ten percent.
КАРОЛИНА	Сколько стоило?	How much did it cost?
МАРК	4000 рублей. И я оставил ещё 100 рублей на чай.	4000 rubles. And I left another 100 rubles for a tip.
ОФИЦИАНТ	Благодарю вас.	I thank you.

In most restaurants, a service charge of ten to twenty percent is included in the bill. You might want to round off the final charge as a tip, or as Russians say **на чай** ("for tea").

(priYATnava)   *(apiTIta)*

Приятного аппетита!

Bon appetit!

You have just returned from Russia and all of your friends are coming for dinner tonight. You have promised them a real Russian meal with all the trimmings. Draw up a menu of what you plan to serve them.

закуски	_____	второе	_____
	_____	овощи	_____
салат	_____	сладкое	_____
суп	_____	напитки	_____
	_____		_____

If you want to get an idea of the choices available to you in Moscow and St Petersburg restaurants go to the site http://www.restoran.ru/

HOW ARE WE DOING?

(KAK) (MY) (DYElaim)

Как мы делаем?

You're already half-way through and you have certainly learned a lot. Now you might want to go back over the first fifteen chapters and do a careful review of all the material we have covered.

In the next few pages you'll find some exercises designed to show you how much you can already accomplish in Russian.

Давайте начнём! Now let's begin!

Can you read the following Russian signs? Look at them carefully and then write the meaning for each sign in the space next to it.

1. **РЕСТОРАН** _____

2. **АЭРОПОРТ** _____

3. **ЖЕНСКИЙ** _____

4. **НЕ КУРИТЬ** _____

5. **ЦЕНТР** _____

Respond to the following questions and courtesy expressions by matching the forms in column **A** with those in column **B**.

<u>**A**</u>

1. Как вас зовут?

2. Спасибо.

3. Сколько стоит эта книга?

4. Который сейчас час?

5. Какая сегодня погода?

<u>**B**</u>

а. Пожалуйста.

б. Книга стоит пятьсот рублей.

в. Сейчас уже десять часов.

г. Сегодня тепло.

д. Меня зовут Иван Попов.

ANSWERS

Matching 1. д 2. а 3. б 4. в 5. г

Signs 1. RESTAURANT 2. AIRPORT 3. LADIES 4. NO SMOKING 5. CENTER

Can you recognize the gender of nouns and replace them with the proper pronouns? Read the first sentence carefully and then fill in the blank space with the correct form of the pronouns **он, она, оно, они**.

1. **Это моя книга.** ________________ **новая.**
2. **Где наш автобус?** **Вот** ________________ **идёт.**
3. **Это ваша газета?** **Нет,** ________________ **не моя.**
4. **Наши стюардессы — русские?** **Да,** ________________ **живут в Москве.**
5. **Где моё письмо?** **Я не знаю, где** ________________ **.**

Do you know all of the words with the letter **«а»** in our word puzzle? Look at the pictures and then fill in the blanks.

ANSWERS

Pronouns 1. Она 2. он 3. она 4. они 5. оно

Puzzle рыба, туалет, магазин, паспорт, банк

Let's see how well you know your numbers in Russian. Do the following simple mathematical equations and fill in the blanks with the written forms of the numerals.

а. 10 _____ – 8 _____ = _____ (_____)

б. 3 _____ + 4 _____ = _____ (_____)

в. 6 _____ – 5 _____ = _____ (_____)

Now let's tell time in Russian. Examine the clocks and fill in the blanks below.

Который сейчас час?

Сейчас _____   _____   _____

How well do you know how to form the **present tense** forms of verbs? Can you construct correct Russian sentences? Fill in the blanks below with the correct endings of the verbs. Remember that the verb form is determined by the subject of the sentence.

1. **Наш отец работа** _____ **в Москве.**

2. **Нина и Борис жив** _____ **в Санкт-Петербурге.**

3. **Мы завтрака** _____ **в шесть часов.**

4. **Я отдыха** _____ **вечером и в субботу.**

5. **Как вы ед** _____ **?**   **На Красной Стреле?**

How good are you at recognizing flags and nationalities? It's not as hard as it seems. Look at the names below and check the flag to identify the proper nation.

1. **Я украинец.**   **Моя страна** _____

2. **Каролина американка.**   **Её страна** _____

3. **Мы русские.**   **Наша страна** _____

4. **Он англичанин.**   **Его страна** _____

5. **Они беларусы.**   **Их страна** _____

Can you tell what the weather will be like in **Москва** and the surrounding areas? Look at the questions first and then find the answers in the weather report below.

1. What kind of weather is expected on December 18?

   a. snowy   **б.** rainy   **в.** sunshine

2. What is the high temperature (in Celsius, of course) for December 18?

   a. $-3°$ **б.** $+5°$ **в.** $-7°$

3. How cold will it get during the night of December 18?

   a. $-2°$ **б.** $-5°$ **в.** $-7°$

4. It will be chilly on December 19. What is the daytime high?

   a. $-3°$ **б.** $-2°$ **в.** $-7°$

5. What can you tell your friends about the weather on December 19?

   a. snow flurries   **б.** rain   **в.** sunshine

В Москве 18 декабря сохранится тёплая погода. Ночью температура от –2 до 0 градусов, днём максимальная температура от +3 до +5, дождь. 19 декабря ночью от –8 до –5 градусов, днём от –5 до –2 градусов, небольшой снег.

Do you recognize what our friends are doing for recreation? Choose from the following list to fill in the blanks with the correct form of the verb corresponding to the scenes below. **(обедать, любить, купаться, отдыхать, бегать)**

1. Каролина _____ .

2. Вечером они всегда _____ в ресторане.

3. Марк _____ .

4. Мы очень _____ русскую оперу.

5. Где и как ты _____ ?

Could you order a meal in a Russian restaurant? Fill in the blanks with the correct word from the list below.

(икра, борщ, рыба, кофе, мороженое, вино, курица)

1. Вы возьмёте суп?   Да, я очень люблю

   русский _____ .

2. Вам нравится _____ ?   У нас и чёрная и красная.

3. На второе я возьму _____ ,

   а мой муж возьмёт _____ .

ANSWERS

Recreation 1. бегает **2.** обедают **3.** купается **4.** любим **5.** отдыхаешь
Food 1. борщ **2.** икра **3.** рыбу, мясо

128

4. Нам очень нравится красное _____ . Принесите
нам ещё одну бутылку.

5. На сладкое мы возьмём _____ ,

а пить будем _____ .

Here is a Russian **кроссворд** with words chosen from the chapters on transportation and eating. See how many you can get.

Кроссворд
Crossword puzzle

По горизонтали
ACROSS

1. bus
4. fork
6. caviar
7. subway
8. knife
9. salt
14. trolley bus
16. vodka

По вертикали
DOWN

2. taxi
3. airplane
4. wine
5. spoon
10. train
11. bread
12. soup
13. meat
15. fish

ANSWERS

Food 4. вино **5.** мороженое, кофе

Crossword puzzle

ACROSS 1. автобус **4.** вилка **6.** икра **7.** метро **8.** нож **9.** соль
14. троллейбус **16.** водка
DOWN 2. такси **3.** самолёт **4.** вино **5.** ложка **10.** поезд **11.** хлеб
12. суп **13.** мясо **15.** рыба

AT THE STORE

(v) (magaZInye)
В магазине

(aDYEZHda)   *(razMYEry)*   *(tsviTA)*
Одежда, Размеры, Цвета
Clothing   Sizes   Colors

(ON) (adiVAitsya)
Он одевается.
He is getting dressed.

(oNA) (razdiVAitsya)
Она раздевается.
She is undressing.

(ON) (nadiVAit)   *(ruBASHku)*
Он надевает рубашку.
He is putting on his shirt.

(oNA) (sniMAit)   *(kambiNAtsiyu)*
Она снимает комбинацию.
She is taking off her slip.

(SHTO)   *(NUZHna)*   *(ZNAT)*
Что нужно знать.
What you need to know.

     In most Russian shops you will first want to examine the articles with the help of the salesperson behind the counter. You may want to ask them to show you an item — **Покажите, пожалуйста** (Show me, please). You may want to try something on — **Можно примерить?** (May I try it on?) When you have finally decided on your purchase you will need to find out the total price — **Сколько стоит?** (How much does it cost?) Then you must go to the cashier and tell him or her the total cost and in which section of the store the item is found. After paying you will receive a receipt (**чек**) which you bring back to the original counter where your purchase will be waiting for you. If you feel unsure of the Russian number system, you might want to have the salesperson write down the price for you. If you smile and show courtesy and good humor, you are likely to be helped through the process.

МУЖСКАЯ ОДЕЖДА

(muSHKAya) *(aDYEZHda)*

Men's clothing

(naSKI)
носки
socks

(ruBASHka)
рубашка
shirt

(pal'TO)
пальто
overcoat

(GALstuk)
галстук
necktie

(truSY)
трусы
underpants

(nasaVOY) *(plaTOK)*
носовой платок
handkerchief

(SVItir)
свитер
sweater

(BRYUki)
брюки
slacks

(MAYka)
майка
undershirt

(pidZHAK)
пиджак
sport coat

(ZONT)
зонт
umbrella

(kaSTYUM)
костюм
suit

(SHLYApa)
шляпа
hat

(sapaGI)
сапоги
boots

(riMYEN')
ремень
belt

(pirCHATki)
перчатки
gloves

(SHTO) *(MNYE)* *(NUZHna)*

Что мне нужно?

What do I need?

When you need something (or someone) in Russian, you must use a form of **нужно.** Literally, the Russians are saying: *Something is necessary to me.* The form of **нужно** will change according to the subject, which is the thing needed. Look at the following examples.

(MNYE) *(NUzhin)* *(NOvy)* *(kaSTYUM)*
Мне нужен новый костюм.   I need a new suit.

(MNYE) *(nuzhNA)* *(NOvaya)* *(SHLYApa)*
Мне нужна новая шляпа.   I need a new hat.

(MNYE) *(NUZHna)* *(NOvaye)* *(pal'TO)*
Мне нужно новое пальто.   I need a new coat.

(MNYE) *(nuzhNY)* *(NOviye)* *(BRYUki)*
Мне нужны новые брюки.   I need new pants.

Now try to tell the salesperson what you need.

1. **Здравствуйте. Мне ——————————— новый зонт.**

2. **Извините, пожалуйста. Мне ——————————— новая рубашка.**

3. **Скажите, пожалуйста, где здесь сапоги. Нам ——————————— сапоги.**

4. **Покажите нам ваши галстуки. Мне ——————————— модный галстук.**

5. **Как вы думаете, мне ——————————— новое пальто?**

When you shop for clothes in Russia you must be aware that there

(ROST)
are great variations in sizes. It is helpful if you know your height (**рост**), chest
(abKHVAT) *(GRUdi)*   *(abKHVAT)* *(TAlii)*
(**обхват груди**) and waist (**обхват талии**) measurements in centimeters in order

to use the conversion charts found in many department and clothing stores. In any

case, you should be sure to try on the item. Ask for the changing booths —
(priMYErachniye) *(kaBIny)*
примерочные кабины.

ANSWERS

Need 1. нужен 2. нужна 3. нужны 4. нужен 5. нужно

Mark's suitcase has been misplaced on the flight to Moscow. He needs a complete set of clothes for his business meetings. Let's see how he does at the **универсальный магазин** *(univirSAL'ny)* *(magaZIN)* (department store).

ПРОДАВЩИЦА (Salesclerk)	**Как можно вам помочь?**	How may I help you?
MARK	**Мне нужно всё — новый костюм, рубашка, и галстук.**	I need everything — a new suit, shirt, and tie.
ПРОДАВЩИЦА	**Хорошо. А что ещё? Носки, трусы, майки?**	Fine. And what else? Socks, underpants, undershirts?
MARK	**Да. Можно примерить брюки и пиджак?**	Yes. May I try on the pants and the jacket?
ПРОДАВЩИЦА	**Конечно. Примерочная кабина вон там.**	Certainly. The changing room is over there.
MARK	**Это не мой размер, и** *(tSVYET)* **цвет мне не нравится.**	This isn't my size, and I don't like the color.
ПРОДАВЩИЦА	**Может быть, этот** *(siDIT)* **сидит лучше?**	Maybe this one fits better?
MARK	*(PRAvy)* **Да. Вы правы.**	Yes. You're right.
ПРОДАВЩИЦА	**Нет. Вы правы.** *(pakuPAtil')* **Покупатель всегда прав.**	No. You're right. The customer is always right.
MARK	**Я возьму всё.** *(paschiTAYtye)* **Подсчитайте, пожалуйста, сколько это стоит.**	I'll take everything. Please, figure up how much it costs.

ПРОДАВЩИЦА	С удовольствием.	With pleasure.
	(zavirNUT) **Вам завернуть?**	Should it be wrapped for you?
MARK	*(naDYEnu)* **Нет. Я всё надену на себя. Спасибо и до свидания.**	No. I'll wear it all. Thank you and goodbye.

(Obuf') ОБУВЬ

Shoes

(tiSNY)
Они мне тесны.
They are too narrow.

(ZHMUT)
Они мне жмут.
They pinch me.

(viliKI)
Они мне велики.
They are too large.

(shiraKI)
Они мне широки.
They're too wide for me.

(sapaGI)
сапоги

(TUfli)
туфли

(baTINki)
ботинки

ЖЕНСКАЯ ОДЕЖДА

(ZHENskaya) *(aDYEZHda)*

Women's clothing

Основные цвета

(asnavNIye) *(tsviTA)*

Basic colors

(ZHOLty) *(byustGAL'tir)*
жёлтый бюстгальтер
yellow bra

(CHORnaya) *(SUMka)*
чёрная сумка
black handbag

(galuBOye) *(PLAt'ye)*
голубое платье
light blue dress

(SIni) *(SHARF)*
синий шарф
dark blue scarf

(ZHOLtiye) *(TRUsiki)*
жёлтые трусики
yellow panties

(BYElaya) *(kambiNAtsiya)*
белая комбинация
white slip

(ziLYOnaya) *(BLUSka)*
зелёная блузка
green blouse

(KRASnaya) *(YUPka)*
красная юбка
red skirt

You and a friend are going to a masquerade ball and want some clothes that really stand out. Write out your order beforehand and then tell the shopkeeper exactly what you need.

Здравствуйте. Мы идём на маскарад, и нам нужны следующие вещи:

следующие — following   items

1. a yellow blouse _____

2. a green tie _____

3. a light blue jacket _____

4. dark blue pants _____

5. red boots _____

6. a black shirt _____

ANSWERS

Clothes 1. жёлтая блузка **2.** зелёный галстук **3.** голубой пиджак **4.** синие брюки **5.** красные сапоги **6.** чёрная рубашка

135

17   *(gastraNOM)* **Гастроном**
The Supermarket

The local **гастроном** (supermarket) may have all or at least some of your needs. You may also see signs for individual shops. Learning them now will help you recognize the stores you'll want to visit.

(malaKO) **молоко** milk	*(MYAsa)* **мясо** meat	*(Ovaschi)* **овощи** vegetables	*(FRUKty)* **фрукты** fruits	*(BUlachnaya)* **булочная** bakery

(RYba) **рыба** fish market	*(kanFYEty)* **конфеты** candy store	*(kanDItirskaya)* **кондитерская** pastry shop	*(maROzhinaye)* **мороженое** ice cream shop	*(vino)* **вино** wine store

(SLISHkam) *(MNOga)* *(vaPROsaf)*
Слишком много вопросов
Too many questions

Mark and Caroline approach a **милиционер** (policeman).

MARK	**Можно вам задать вопрос?**	May I ask you a question?
МИЛИЦИОНЕР	**Слушаю вас.**	I'm listening.
MARK	**Где можно купить хлеб?**	Where can I buy bread?

136

МИЛИЦИОНЕР	Булочная на этой улице.	The bakery is on this street.
CAROLINE	Где можно купить шампанское?	Where can I buy champagne?
МИЛИЦИОНЕР	В магазине «ВИНО»	In the liquor store.
CAROLINE	А где можно купить масло и кефир?	Where can one buy butter and kefir?
МИЛИЦИОНЕР	В магазине «МОЛОКО».	In the dairy store.
MARK	Где овощи и фрукты?	Where are the vegetables and fruits?
МИЛИЦИОНЕР	В магазине «ОВОЩИ» и «ФРУКТЫ», или на рынке. *(RYNkye)*	In the vegetable and fruit store, or at the market.
CAROLINE	А где можно найти *(nayTI)* говядину и свинину? *(gaVYAdinu) (sviNInu)*	Where can one find beef and pork?
МИЛИЦИОНЕР	В магазине «МЯСО».	In the meat store.
MARK	Я люблю торт. Где . . . ?	I love cake. Where is . . . ?
МИЛИЦИОНЕР	В кондитерской.	In the pastry shop.
CAROLINE	А где кофе, и чай, и лимонад, и вино?	And where is the coffee, and the tea, and the soda, and the wine?
МИЛИЦИОНЕР	Хватит! Вы задаёте слишком много вопросов. *(KHVAtit) (zadaYOtye)*	That's enough! You're asking too many questions.
MARK	Какой несимпатичный милиционер!	What an unfriendly policeman!
CAROLINE	Нет, Марк, он прав. Это было действительно много вопросов. *(diystVItil'na)*	No, Mark, he's right. That was really a lot of questions.

Read the following statements about Mark and Caroline's conversation and write **правда** (true) or **неправда** (false) in the blanks.

1. Хлеб можно найти в булочной. _____

2. Масло можно купить в магазине «ВИНО». _____

3. Шампанское можно найти в магазине «ФРУКТЫ». _____

4. Говядину можно купить в магазине «МЯСО». _____

5. Торт можно найти в кондитерской. _____

(SKOL'ka)   *(VYEsit)*

Сколько весит?

How much does it weigh?

Although the metric system is widely used for measurements in Russia and in other countries and has become increasingly more familiar to Americans, it is still useful to examine how Russians order items in their shops.

100 грамм	100 grams = 3.5 ounces
200 грамм	200 grams = 7 ounces (almost ½ pound)
500 грамм, полкило	500 grams, half a kilo = 17.5 ounces (one pound + 1.5 ounces)
1000 грамм, 1 килограмм	1000 grams, one kilogram = 2.205 pounds
1 литр	1 liter = 1.06 quarts

(SKOL'ka)   *(STOit)*

Сколько стоит?

How much does it cost?

Read aloud the names of the different sorts of containers that food can come in. Then ask the clerk how much the items cost.

Сколько стоит . . . ?

(kuSOK) (MYla)
кусок мыла
bar of soap

(BANka) (KOfye)
банка кофе
jar of coffee

(diSYAtak) (yalTS)
десяток яиц
ten eggs

(LITR) (malaKA)
литр молока
a liter of milk

(paKYET) (muKI)
пакет муки
package of flour

(STO) (GRAM) (SYra)
сто грамм сыра
100 grams of cheese

(kaROPka) (kanFYET)
коробка конфет
a box of candy

(ruLON) (tuaLYETnay) (buMAgi)
рулон туалетной бумаги
a roll of toilet paper

(baTON) (BYElava)(KHLYEba)
батон белого хлеба
a loaf of white bread

(PACHka) (SAkhara)
пачка сахара
a bag of sugar

(buTYLka) (viNA)
бутылка вина
a bottle of wine

(kilaGRAM) (karTOSHki)
килограмм картошки
a kilogram of potatoes

THE GENITIVE CASE

We have seen several instances where Russians use the **genitive case** when they describe a container or measure of something: a liter of, a package of, a box of, a bottle of, etc. The item contained in the package is rendered in Russian in the **genitive case**. Look at the way the **genitive case** is formed.

For masculine nouns that end in a hard consonant, and neuter nouns ending in **o**, the genitive case is formed by the addition of the ending **a**.

<u>Nominative</u>   <u>Genitive</u>

                                                  loaf of bread
хлеб   **батон хлеба**

                                                  bottle of milk
молоко   **бутылка молока**

If there is a soft consonant, such as **й**, or a soft sign **ь** ending for masculine nouns, or the ending **e** for neuter nouns, change the ending to **я**.

                                                  package of tea
чай   **пачка чая**

For feminine nouns ending in **a**, change the **a** to **ы**.

                                                  kilogram of fish
рыба   **килограмм рыбы**

If the noun ends in **я**, it changes to **и**. Also observe the spelling rule that requires us to write **и**, not **ы** after the letters **к, г, х, ш, щ, ж, ч**.

                                                  roll of paper
бумага   **рулон бумаги**

Let's see if you can ask the clerk for the following items. Be sure to put the item in the **genitive case**.

Дайте мне, пожалуйста . . .   (Please give me . . .)

1. (a bottle of beer)   **пиво**   **бутылку** _____ .

2. (a can of soup)   **суп**   **банку** _____ .

3. (100 grams of vodka)   **водка**   **сто грамм** _____ .

4. (a kilogram of fish)   **рыба**   **килограмм** _____ .

5. (a package of tea)   **чай**   **пачку** _____ .

(RYnak)
РЫНОК
The market

One place you should not overlook in your shopping is the **рынок**. These marketplaces are almost always better stocked than the stores, and they offer a feast of sights and smells. The local farmers are eager to sell their wares and will enter into lively conversations as they let you sample their goods. Be sure to bring a plastic or net bag to carry home your purchases. Russians even have a special word for this bag you take along "just in case" — **авоська** *(aVOS'ka)*.

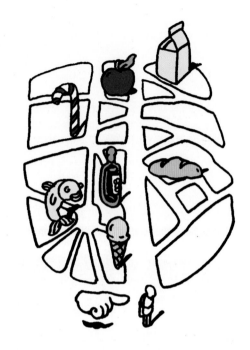

Куда надо идти?

It's your turn to do the shopping. Which way must you go to get all of the items at the right? Do you remember the words for directions?

прямо	straight ahead
направо	to the right
налево	to the left

You are standing near the ice cream shop. Fill in the blanks as you move from one shop to the next.

Сперва я иду _____ купить мороженое. Потом мне надо купить рыбу и я

иду _____ . Мои дети хотят конфеты, поэтому я иду _____ .

Потом я иду _____ , где я всегда покупаю овощи и фрукты. Чтобы

купить молоко, мне надо идти _____ и _____ . Уже поздно,

но нам ещё нужен хлеб. Я иду прямо и _____ в булочную. Это всё?

Нет! Где можно купить вино? Идите _____ . Теперь я могу

идти _____ домой.

If you are looking for toiletries, cosmetics or simple personal needs, you might find them in the hotel lobby at a **киоск** or in a special section of the store called **парфюмерия**. If you have a prescription to be filled you will have to take it to the pharmacy — **аптека**. Let's take a look at some of the names for frequently needed items.

(zubNAya)
зубная щётка
toothbrush

(SCHOTka)
щётка
hairbrush

(ZYERkala)
зеркало
mirror

(zubNAya) (PASta)
зубная паста
toothpaste

(rasCHOSka)
расчёска
comb

(salFYETki)
салфетки
tissues

(LAK) (dlya) (vaLOS)
лак для волос
hairspray

(ruMYAna)
румяна
rouge

(TUSH) (dlya) (risNITS)
тушь для ресниц
mascara

(atsiTON)
ацетон
nail polish remover

ОТДЕЛ «ПАРФЮМЕРИЯ»
(aDYEL) *(parfyuMYEriya)*

The toiletries section

ИРИНА (Irina)	*(KRYEM)* *(liTSA)* **Мне нужен крем для лица.**	I need some face cream.
МАША (Masha)	*(meyk-UP)* **Ты купила мэйк-ап вчера.**	You purchased makeup yesterday.
ИРИНА	**Я знаю, но он мне не** *(paNRAvilsya)* **понравился.**	I know, but I did not like it.
МАША	**Да. И я забыла купить** *(buMAZHniye)* *(pilYONki)* *(TAL'K)* **бумажные пелёнки и тальк.**	Yes. And I forgot to buy disposable diapers and talcum.
КАССИР (Cashier)	**Могу ли я вам помочь?**	May I help you?
МАША	**У вас есть бумажные пелёнки?**	Do you have disposable diapers?
КАССИР	**К сожалению, я продал последний пакет час назад.**	Unfortunately, I sold the last package an hour ago.
МАША	*(duKHI)* **Ничего. А духи у вас** *(daraGIye)* **дорогие?**	That's all right. Are your perfumes expensive?
КАССИР	**Не очень. Вы пробовали наши новые русские духи?**	Not very. Have you tried our new Russian perfume?
ИРИНА	**Я их возьму, и также** *(gubNUyu)* *(paMAdu)* *(TYEni)* **губную помаду, тени и крем для рук.**	I'll take it, and also lipstick, eyeshadow and hand cream.

144

Прошедшее время

The past tense

купить to buy	**купи + ла**	**Ирина купила мэйк-ап.** Irina bought makeup.
забыть to forget	**забы + л**	**Я забыл зубную щётку.** I forgot the toothbrush.
продать to sell	**прода + ли**	**Они продали все духи.** They sold all the perfume.
понравиться to like	**понрави + ло + сь**	**Это нам не понравилось.** We did not like this.

To form the **past tense** of a Russian verb, you drop the **ть** or **ти** ending of the infinitive and in the singular you add **л** for masculine subjects, **ла** for feminine subjects, and **ло** for neuter subjects. For all plurals you add **ли**. When the verb ends in **ся**, form the **past tense** first and then add **ся** after **л**, and **сь** after **ла, ло, ли**.

Now let's see how well you can recognize the past tense in practice. Fill in the blanks with the Russian words **правда** or **неправда.**

1. **Ирина купила мэйк-ап вчера?** _____

2. **Мэйк-ап Маше понравился?** _____

3. **Маша купила бумажные пелёнки?** _____

4. **Кассирша продала последний пакет час назад?** _____

5. **Ирина взяла крем для рук?** _____

Нужные вещи

Necessary items

Write the names of these important items in the blanks provided.

(dizadaRANT)
дезодорант
deodorant

_____

(LYEZviya)
лезвия
razor blades

_____

(elikTRIchiskaya) *(BRITva)*
электрическая бритва
electric shaver

_____

(BRITva)
бритва
razor

_____

When his electric shaver breaks, Alexander discovers that he too has a few items to pick up.

АЛЕКСАНДР	**Моя электрическая бритва** **не работает.**	My electric shaver doesn't work.
КАССИР	**Купите бритву и лезвия.**	Buy a razor and blades.
АЛЕКСАНДР	*(raBOty)* **Это слишком много работы.**	That's too much work.
	(brit'YA) **Крем для бритья,**	Shaving cream,
	(las'YON) **лосьон после бритья.**	aftershave lotion.
КАССИР	*(vizDYE)* **Да. Но она везде** **работает.**	Yes. But it works everywhere.
АЛЕКСАНДР	**Вы правы. И я всегда**	You're right. And I always
	(MYla) *(shamPUN')* **беру мыло и шампунь.**	take soap and shampoo.
КАССИР	*(adikaLON)* **Не забудьте одеколон!**	Don't forget the cologne!

В АПТЕКЕ

At the pharmacy

If you are given a prescription you will need to go to a pharmacy — **Аптека**. Here you can also find non-prescription remedies for what ails you. There is also a *(ritsepTURny)* *(aDYEL)* **Рецептурный отдел** (prescription section). You should ask **Нужен рецепт?** (Is a prescription necessary?) To find out

if they have the proper medicine ask: **У вас есть лекарство по этому рецепту?** Or you may

(lIKARSTva)   *(rITSEPTa)*

simply ask for **лекарства без рецепта** (over the counter medicines).

We hope you won't need to use the following words and phrases, but just in case:

Мне нужно что-нибудь от _____ .

I need something for _____ .

У вас есть _____ ?

Do you have _____ ?

(NASmarka)
насморка
a cold

(PLAStyr')
пластырь
adhesive tape

(zaPOra)
запора
constipation

(SCHOlach)
щёлочь
an antacid

(KASHlya)
кашля
cough

(SPIRT)
спирт
alcohol

(paNOsa)
поноса
diarrhea

(antiSYEPtik)
антисептик
an antiseptic

(ZHAra)
жара
a fever

(aspiRIN)
аспирин
aspirin

(galavNOY)   *(BOli)*
головной боли
a headache

(BINT)
бинт
bandages

(tashnaTY)
тошноты
nausea

(VAta)
вата
cotton

(SOLnichnava)   *(aZHOga)*
солнечного ожога
sunburn

(glazNIye)   *(KApli)*
глазные капли
eyedrops

(zubNOY)   *(BOli)*
зубной боли
a toothache

(YOT)
йод
iodine

(zhiLUdachnava)   *(raSTROYSTva)*
желудочного расстройства
upset stomach

(tirMOmitr)
термометр
a thermometer

Let's make sure that we can get some of the essentials.

Match items in column A with associated words or phrases in column B.

A	B
1. аспирин	а. от желудочного расстройства
2. мэйк-ап	б. лезвия
3. бритва	в. губная помада
4. щёлочь	г. от головной боли

Here is your shopping list. Can you translate the items into Russian for the cashier?

a. shampoo _____

б. deodorant _____

в. face cream _____

г. toothpaste _____

д. rouge _____

ANSWERS

Matching 1. г 2. в 3. б 4. а.
Shopping list а. шампунь б. дезодорант в. крем для лица г. зубная паста
д. румяна

(pastiRAT')
постирать
to wash

(paCHISti')
почистить
to clean

(pasuSHYT')
посушить
to dry

(paGLAdit')
погладить
to iron

You may be able to have your shirts, blouses, and underwear washed at the hotel for a modest price. There will also probably be an ironing board and iron on your floor. Simply inquire at the reception desk. Otherwise, you may want to try out the laundromat and dry cleaner's.

(PRAchichnaya) (samaapSLUzhivaniya)
прачечная самообслуживания
laundromat

(khimCHISTka)
химчистка
dry cleaner's

(paraSHOk) (dlya) (STIRki)
порошок для стирки
soap powder

(glaDIL'naya)   (daSKA)
гладильная доска
ironing board

(uTYUK)
утюг
iron

(stiRAL'naya)   (maSHYna)
стиральная машина
washing machine

СТИРКА И ЧИСТКА В ГОСТИНИЦЕ
Laundry and dry cleaning in the hotel

(GORnichnaya)

The **горничная** (maid) in your hotel will be happy to do your laundry. Here are some useful expressions.

(biL'YO)

Вы можете постирать моё бельё?   Can you wash my underwear?

(priSHEYtye)   (PUgavitsu)

Пришейте, пожалуйста, пуговицу.   Please sew on the button.

(ruKAF)

Вы можете починить этот рукав?   Can you mend this sleeve?

Вы можете погладить рубашку?   Can you iron the shirt?

(nakraKHMAL'tye)

Накрахмальте только немножко.   Just a little starch.

(kaSTYUM)

Вы можете сдать костюм в чистку?   Can you take my suit to the cleaner's?

(VYvisti)   (pitNO)

Вы можете вывести это пятно?   Can you remove this stain?

Now fill in the blanks using the words and expressions found above.

1. **У вас есть** _____ **и** _____ **?**
   an iron   an ironing board

2. **Вы можете** _____ **моё** _____ **?**
   wash   my underwear

3. **Вы можете** _____ **мою** _____ **?**
   an iron   shirt

4. **Вы можете сдать** _____ **в** _____ **?**
   suit   the cleaner's

5. **Вы можете** _____ **это** _____ **?**
   remove   stain

(ZHAlaby)
ЖАЛОБЫ
Complaints

Марк всегда сдаёт бельё горничной в стирку. В этот раз есть маленькая проблема.	Mark always gives his clothes to the maid to be washed. This time there is a small problem.
Он получил не своё бельё.	He received someone else's underwear.
Марк жалуется горничной.	Mark complains to the maid.
Он не носит женское бельё.	He doesn't wear women's underwear.

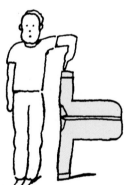

В рубашках слишком много крахмала, двух носков не хватает, один красный носок, и один зелёный.

The shirts have too much starch. Two socks are missing, one red sock, and one green one.

И наконец, в одной рубашке есть дырка.

And finally, in one shirt there's a hole.

Марк очень сердит.

Mark is very angry.

Как вы думаете?

What do you think?

У него есть на что жаловаться?

Does he have something to complain about?

151

Here are some useful phrases if you have a complaint.

(YA) (BUdu) (ZHAlavatsa)
Я буду жаловаться.
I'm going to complain.

(Eta) (NYE) (maYO) (biL'YO)
Это не моё бельё.
This is not my laundry.

(NYE) (khvaTAit) (PUgavitsy)
Не хватает пуговицы.
A button is missing.

(NYE) (khvaTAit) (MAYki)
Не хватает майки.
An undershirt is missing.

(VY) (NYE) (slaZHYli) (ruBASHki)
Вы не сложили рубашки.
You didn't fold the shirts.

(VY) (NYE) (paGLAdili) (YUPku)
Вы не погладили юбку.
You didn't iron the skirt.

Can you fill in the blanks corresponding to the pictures?

1. **Мне надо погладить** _____ .

2. **Мне надо сдать в стирку** _____ .

3. **Вы можете мне пришить** _____ ?

4. **Вы можете сдать в чистку** _____ .

5. **Мне надо постирать** _____ .

ANSWERS

Fill in 1. костюм 2. бельё 3. пуговицу 4. платье 5. носки

20 *(saLOn)* *(krasaTY)* *(parikMAkhirskaya)*
Салон красоты / Парикмахерская
Beauty Salon   Barber Shop

(ZHENski) *(ZAL)*
ЖЕНСКИЙ ЗАЛ
Ladies' salon

(VOlasy)	*(DLIna)*	*(KOratka)*	*(bryuNYETka)*	*(blanDINka)*
волосы	**длинно**	**коротко**	**брюнетка**	**блондинка**
hair	long	short	a brunette	a blond

(myTYO)
мытьё
a shampoo

(SCHOTka)
щётка
brush

(priCHOSka)
причёска
hairdo

(STRISHka)
стрижка
haircut

(uKLATka)
укладка
set

(priCHOsyvat')
причёсывать
to comb

(maniKYUR)
маникюр
manicure

(maSASH) *(liTSA)*
массаж лица
facial massage

(LAK) *(dlya)* *(vaLOS)*
лак для волос
hairspray

(biguDI)
бигуди
rollers

(FYEN)
фен
hair dryer

(NOZHnitsy)
ножницы
scissors

Two women, Dorothy and Joan, decide to go to the beauty shop.

ПАРИКМАХЕР (Hairdresser)	Что вам сделать?	What can I do for you?
JOAN	*(VYmayte)* *(GOlavu)* Вымойте мне голову, и сделайте стрижку и укладку.	I'd like a shampoo, and a cut and set.
ПАРИКМАХЕР	А вам, госпожа?	And for you. Miss?
DOROTHY	Вымойте мне голову, сделайте укладку и маникюр.	I'd like a shampoo, and a set and a manicure.
ПАРИКМАХЕР	*(paKRAsit')* Вам покрасить *(VOlasy)* волосы?	Would you like a color rinse?
DOROTHY	Нет. Не сегодня.	No. Not today, thank you.
ПАРИКМАХЕР	Только поправить?	Just a touch-up?
DOROTHY	Хорошо, но только без лака, пожалуйста.	All right, but no hairspray, please.
ПАРИКМАХЕР	Можно феном? *(vzgliNItye)* Теперь взгляните в зеркало.	May I use the hair dryer? Now look in the mirror.
DOROTHY	Прекрасно. Спасибо.	Marvelous. Thank you.

Here are some useful expressions for the beauty parlor. Repeat them aloud as you write them out.

Можно записаться на завтра?	May I make an appointment for tomorrow?
Сделайте мне модную причёску.	Give me a modern (new) hairdo.
Что-нибудь с кудрями.	Something with curls.
Мне нужно покрасить волосы.	I need a color rinse.

Мытьё и укладку, пожалуйста.	A wash and set, please.
Химическую завивку и тон.	A permanent (wave) and a tint.
Совсем немного лака.	Just a little hairspray.

FOR WOMEN ONLY: You are off to the beauty salon. Do you know what you want? Make a list in Russian just in case.

Мне нужно слелать
I need

1. (a wash) _____
2. (a set) _____
3. (a cut) _____

Мне нужно 4. (a color rinse) _____

(muSHKOY) *(ZAL)*
МУЖСКОЙ ЗАЛ
The barber shop

(parikMAkhir)
парикмахер
barber

(paBRIT')
побрить
shave

(BRITva)
бритва
razor

(paBRItsa)
побриться
shave oneself

(baraDA) (i) (viSOCHki)
борода и височки
beard and sideburns

(uSY)
усы
moustache

(priCHOsyvat')
причёсывать
to comb/brush

(STRISHka)
стрижка
cut

(priCHOsyvatsa)
причёсываться
to comb/brush one's own hair

MARK	**Где хорошая парикмахерская?**	Where is there a good barber shop?
HOTEL CLERK	**Есть парикмахерская в гостинице.**	There's a barber shop in the hotel.
MARK	**Мне долго ждать?**	Do I have to wait long?
ПАРИКМАХЕР (Barber)	**Нет, вы следующий.**	No, you're next.
MARK	**Я хочу постричься и побриться.**	I want a haircut and a shave.
ПАРИКМАХЕР	**Как вас постричь?**	How do you want it cut?
MARK	**Сзади коротко, спереди длинно.**	Short in the back, long in the front.
ПАРИКМАХЕР	**Вам голову помыть?**	Would you like a shampoo?
MARK	**Нет, не надо.**	No, that's not necessary.

ПАРИКМАХЕР	Так хорошо?	Is that all right?
MARK	Можно покороче по бокам.	A little shorter on the sides.
ПАРИКМАХЕР	Вы причёсываетс волосы прямо назад?	Do you comb your hair straight back?
MARK	Нет, у меня пробор налево.	No, I have a part on the left.
ПАРИКМАХЕР	Вам одеколон?	Would you like some cologne?
MARK	Пожалуйста.	Please.
	Сколько с меня?	How much do I owe you?

Где хорошая парикмахерская?   Where is there a good barber shop?

_____

Мне долго ждать?   Do I have long to wait?

_____

Я хочу постричься.   I would like a haircut.

_____

Я хочу побриться.   I would like a shave.

_____

Подстригите немножко сверху.   Cut a little off the top.

_____

Подправьте, пожалуйста, усы.   Please trim the moustache.

_____

Ножницами, или только бритвой?   With the scissors or a razor cut?

_____

(gaZYETny)   *(kiOSK)*
Газетный киоск
The Newsstand

(kantsiLYARskie)   *(taVAry)*
Канцелярские товары
Stationery Goods/Office Supplies

(u)   *(gaZYETnava)*   *(kiOSka)*
У ГАЗЕТНОГО КИОСКА
At the newsstand

English-language newspapers and magazines may be available at the hotel newsstand. At these and other stands throughout the cities you can also purchase stamps, postcards, envelopes, maps of the city, and the little lapel pins — **значки** — that make fine souvenirs.

(zhurNAL)
журнал
magazine

(gaZYEta)
газета
newspaper

(atKRYTki)
открытки
postcards

(MARki)
марки
stamps

(sigaRYEty)
сигареты
cigarettes

CAROLINE	У вас есть газеты	Do you have newspapers
	(anGLIYskam) *(yizyKYE)* на английском языке?	in English?
SALESCLERK	Да. И вот ещё	Yes. And here are some
	журналы на английском.	magazines in English.
CAROLINE	*(kuPIT)* Я хочу купить эти	I would like to buy these
	открытки.	postcards.
SALESCLERK	Вам нужны марки?	Do you need stamps?
CAROLINE	Нет. У меня есть.	No. I have some.
	Сколько стоит этот	How much does that
	(znaCHOK) значок?	pin cost?

SALESCLERK	Двадцать рублей. А здесь *(naBOR)* красивый набор наших *(FLAgof)* флагов за 100 рублей.	Twenty rubles. But here is a beautiful set of our flags for one hundred rubles.
CAROLINE	Хорошо. Я возьму один набор.	Fine. I'll take one set.
SALESCLERK	Ещё что-нибудь?	Anything else?
CAROLINE	Спасибо. Это всё. Я почти забыла. У вас есть американские сигареты?	Thank you. That's everything. I almost forgot. Do you have any American cigarettes?
SALESCLERK	К сожалению, *(rasPROdany)* все распроданы.	Unfortunately, they were all sold out.

Read through the conversation several times and review the new words you will need. Then see if you can write down the necessary words in Russian for your friend who is going out for a few items. He has written them down in English. Can you provide the Russian?

1. stamps _____

2. postcards _____

3. cigarettes _____

4. a lapel pin _____

(f) *(kantsiLYARskam)* В КАНЦЕЛЯРСКОМ ОТДЕЛЕ *(aDYElye)*

At the stationery store

Here are some of the items you might want to purchase at the stationery store. Say them aloud and then write out the words in the spaces provided.

(karanDASH)
карандаш
pencil

_____

(kanVYERT)
конверт
envelope

_____

(RUCHka)
ручка
pen

_____

(SKOTCH)
скотч
transparent tape

_____

(shpaGAT)
шпагат
string

_____

(tiTRAT)
тетрадь
notebook

_____

(blakNOT)
блокнот
writing pad

_____

(buMAga) (dlya) (PIsim)
бумага для писем
writing paper

_____

Here is a short paragraph to study about Oleg's trip to the newsstand.

Вчера вечером я хотел **писать письмо** сыну и дочке. **Сперва я пошёл в магазин** «Канцелярские товары», где я купил **блокнот** и конверты. **После того как я написал** письма, я пошёл в киоск. Там я купил марки, **несколько** открыток, **и пачку сигарет.** По пути домой **я съел** мороженое и купил хлеб и молоко.	Last evening I wanted to write a letter to my son and daughter. First I went to the stationery store where I purchased a writing pad and envelopes. After I had written the letters, I went to the newsstand. There I purchased stamps, several postcards, and a pack of cigarettes. On the way home I ate some ice cream and bought bread and milk.

Now read through the Russian text again aloud without looking at the English. Can you trace Oleg's route from start to finish on the map below?

Now let's end with a word search. Find and circle the Russian equivalents for the following words: **envelope, postcard, stamps, pencil, pen, newspaper, writing pad.** When you have found all of the words, write them in the spaces below.

а	б	р	г	а	з	е	т	а	д
з	л	у	к	о	н	в	е	р	т
м	о	о	а	т	р	с	ы	ф	х
а	к	а	р	а	н	д	а	ш	щ
р	н	х	д	з	п	н	м	л	к
к	о	т	к	р	ы	т	к	а	ю
и	т	я	щ	р	у	ч	к	а	щ

_____   _____

_____   _____

_____

(yuviLIRniye)   *(izDYEliya)*
Ювелирные изделия
Jewelry Articles

(chiSY)
Часы
Watches

(yuviLIRny)   *(magaZIN)*
Ювелирный магазин
The jewelry store

(braSLYET)
браслет
bracelet

(BROSH)
брошь
brooch

(azhiRYEl'e)
ожерелье
necklace

(tsiPOCHka)
цепочка
chain

(kal'TSO)
кольцо
ring

(SYER'gi)
серьги
earrings

(kal'TSO) *(s)* *(KAMnim)*
кольцо с камнем
ring with precious stone

Mark goes to a jewelry store to buy a gift for his wife.

SALESCLERK	**Как вам помочь?**	How may I help you?
MARK	**Я хочу купить жене**	I would like to buy something
	что-нибудь.	for my wife.
SALESCLERK	*(MOzhit)* **Браслет, или может**	A bracelet, or perhaps
	(BYT') *(siRYEbrinaye)* **быть серебряное кольцо?**	a silver ring?

MARK	**Нет. Она предпочитает** *(ZOlata)* **золото.**	No. She prefers gold.
SALESCLERK	**Как вам нравится эта** *(PAlikha)* **брошь из Палеха?**	How do you like this brooch from Palekh?
MARK	**Она очень красива.** *(yintaRYOM)* **И эти серьги с янтарём** **тоже очень красивы.**	It's beautiful. And these amber earrings are lovely too.
SALESCLERK	**Да. И у нас есть** *(padkhaDYAscheye)* **подходящее ожерелье.**	Yes. And we have a matching necklace.
MARK	**Прекрасно. Сколько** *(VMYEStye)* **они стоят вместе?**	Fine. How much do they cost together?
SALESCLERK	**Две тысячи рублей.**	Two thousand rubles.
MARK	**Вы думаете, что я** *(baGAty)* **богатый американец?**	What do you think, that I am a rich American?
SALESCLERK	**Нет. Но вы совсем не** *(BYEDny)* **бедный русский!**	No. But you are certainly not a poor Russian either!
MARK	**Тогда я их возьму.** **Они дорогие, но** *(paDYElayish)* **что поделаешь?**	In that case I'll take them. They're expensive, but what can you do?

Some of your relatives back home have expensive tastes and want you to bring them a piece of jewelry from Russia. Can you make out your list in Russian?

1. Aunt Dottie would like a brooch. _____

2. Grandma wants some earrings. _____

3. Your daughter-in-law wants a ring. _____

4. Grandpa wants a bracelet for his new girlfriend. _____

5. You only need a chain for your watch. _____

ANSWERS

Jewelry 1. брошь 2. серьги 3. кольцо 4. браслет 5. цепочка

(dragaTSEnye)   *(KAMni)*

Драгоценные камни

Precious stones

Pronounce the words below aloud and write them out in the spaces provided.

(briliANT)
бриллиант
diamond

(ZHEMchuk)
жемчуг
pearl

(saPFIR)
сапфир
sapphire

_____

_____

_____

(izuMRUT)
изумруд
emerald

(ruBIN)
рубин
ruby

(yanTAR')
янтарь
amber

_____

_____

_____

(ZOlata)
золото
gold

(PLAtina)
платина
platinum

(siriBRO)
серебро
silver

_____

_____

_____

Do you remember the adjectives for colors in Russian? See if you can match the following color adjectives with the names of the precious stones that they modify.

1. зелёный

2. белый

3. красный

4. жёлтый

5. синий

а. сапфир

б. изумруд

в. жемчуг

г. рубин

д. янтарь

ANSWERS

Matching 1.б 2.в 3.г 4.д 5.а

164

(chiSY)
ЧАСЫ
Watches/Clocks

(buDIL'nik)
будильник
alarm clock

(naRUCHniye) (chiSY)
наручные часы
wristwatch

(karMAniye)   (chiSY)
карманные часы
pocket watch

(riMONT) (chiSOF)
ремонт часов
watch repair shop

Practice saying aloud and writing the words from the sentences below. Read them over again until you feel comfortable with the expressions you will need to get your watch repaired.

Can you repair this watch?
Вы можете починить эти часы?

_____

Can you clean it?
Можно их почистить?

_____

My watch is fast.
Мои часы спешат.

My watch is slow.
Мои часы отстают.

_____

My watch has stopped running.
Мои часы стоят.

My watch doesn't run well.
Мои часы плохо идут.

_____

I wind it every day.
Я завожу их каждый день.

_____

Can you put in a new battery?
Можно поставить новую батарейку?

_____

Note that the Russian word for watch or clock is **часы** (hours) and is plural. Therefore it requires a plural form of the verb.

Try to select the correct word(s) to fill in the blanks below.

Ремонт часов, спешат, плохо идут, отстают, батарейку.

1. **Когда мои часы** _____ **, я прихожу рано.**   (I arrive early.)

2. **Когда мои часы** _____ **, я опаздываю.**   (I am late.)

3. **Когда мои часы стоят, я иду в магазин** _____

4. **Когда мои часы** _____ **,**

5.   **можно поставить новую** _____ **.**

(fotaapaRAty)
Фотоаппараты
Cameras

(paDArak)
подарок
gift

(samaVAR)
самовар
samovar

(shkaTULka)
шкатулка
lacquer box

(maTRYOSHka)
матрёшка
nested doll

(balaLAYka)
балалайка
balalaika

(mikhaVAya) *(SHAPka)*
меховая шапка
fur hat

(diriVYAnaya) *(paSUda)*
деревянная посуда
wooden dishes

(iGRUSHka)
игрушка
toy

(plaTOK)
платок
shawl

Make sure you visit the gift shop before you leave. Read carefully how Mark goes shopping for his friends and family back home.

MARK

Я хотел бы купить   I would like to purchase

(NYEskal'ka)
несколько сувениров.   some souvenirs.

ПРОДАВЩИЦА	Вам нужны типичные *(tiPICHniye)* русские сувениры?	You need real Russian souvenirs?
MARK	Да, как самовар, или матрёшка.	Yes, like a samovar, or a nested doll.
ПРОДАВЩИЦА	У нас красивые балалайки, и деревянные ложки. *(LOSHki)*	We have lovely balalaikas, and wooden spoons.
MARK	Сколько стоит эта меховая шапка?	How much does this fur hat cost?
ПРОДАВЩИЦА	Она дорогая. *(daraGAya)* Это настоящая норка. *(NORka)*	It is expensive. It is real mink.
MARK	Может быть я возьму эту палехскую *(PAlikhskuyu)* шкатулку?	Maybe I'll take this Palekh lacquer box.
ПРОДАВЩИЦА	Хорошо. Она хотя не дешёвая, но и не *(diSHOvaya)* слишком дорогая.	Good. Although it is not inexpensive, it is not too expensive.
MARK	Можно платить кредитной карточкой? *(kriDITnay) (KARtachkay)*	May I pay with a credit card?
ПРОДАВЩИЦА	Конечно. Вам завернуть? *(zavirNUT)*	Of course. Should I wrap it for you?

1. Марк хочет купить русские сувениры. _____

2. Меховая шапка не очень дорогая. _____

3. Самовар настоящий русский сувенир. _____

4. Палехская шкатулка слишком дешёвая. _____

5. Марк хочет платить кредитной карточкой. _____

(magaZIN) (MUzyka)
МАГАЗИН–МУЗЫКА
The music store

(kaSYEta)
кассета
cassette tape

(kamPAKTny) (DISK)
компактный диск
CD (compact disc)

(plaSTINka)
пластинка
record

(videokaSYEta)
видеокассета
videocassette

(naRODnaya) (MUzyka)
народная музыка
folk music

(klaSIchiskaya) (MUzyka)
классическая музыка
classical music

(savriMYEnaya) (MUzyka)
современная музыка
pop (contemporary) music

(RAdio)
радио
radio

(tiliVIzar)
телевизор
television

(PLYEyir)
mp3-плеер
mp3-player

ANSWERS
True or false 1. правда 2. неправда 3. правда 4. неправда 5. правда

(kamPYUtir)
компьютер
computer

(NOTbuk)
ноутбук
laptop/computer

(mikraFON)
микрофон
microphone

Try to read aloud the following paragraph that will come in handy if you enjoy listening to music.

Мама и папа очень любят музыку.

Mom and Dad like music very much.

Когда они были в Москве, они

When they were in Moscow, they

ходили в магазин «Музыка».

went to the music store.

Там мама хотела купить

There Mom wanted to buy

классическую музыку, Чайковский,

classical music, Tchaikovsky,

Римский-Корсаков, Бородин.

Rimsky-Korsakov, Borodin.

Она купила компактные диски.

She bought some CDs.

У неё есть CD-плеер.

She has a CD-player.

Папа любит русскую народную музыку,

Papa likes Russian folk music,

и он купил mp3-плеер.

and he bought an mp3-player.

Теперь в нашем доме

Now in our house

можно всё время

you can listen all the time

слушать русскую музыку.

to Russian music.

Read over the dialogue one more time and then try to write out the words in the missing blanks.

1. **Мама хотела купить** _____ **музыку.**

2. **Она купила** _____ .

3. **Папа любит русскую** _____ **музыку.**

4. **Он купил** _____ .

5. **Теперь в нашем доме можно слушать** _____ **музыку.**

ANSWERS

(fotataVAry)
ФОТОТОВАРЫ
Photographic supplies

(fotaKARtachka)
фотокарточка
print

(fotaapaRAT)
фотоаппарат
camera

(batiREYka)
батарейка
battery

(KARta) (PAmyati)
карта памяти
memory card

(PLYONka)
плёнка
film

(videoKAmira)
видеокамера
video camera

At the photo counter Caroline tries to get her film developed.

CAROLINE	*(napiCHAtat')* **Здесь можно напечатать фотографии?**	Can one print photos here?
CLERK	*(napiCHAtat')* **Да. Вам напечатать все?**	Yes. Should I print them all?
CAROLINE	**Да, тридцать шесть кадров.**	Yes, thirty-six exposures.
CLERK	*(CHORna- BYEliye)* *(tsvitNIye)* **Чёрно-белые или цветные?**	Black-and-white or color?
CAROLINE	*(uviLIchit')* **Цветные, и можно увеличить.**	Color, and you can enlarge them.
CLERK	*(GLYANtsiviye)* *(MAtaviye)* **Глянцевые или матовые?**	Glossy or matte finish?
CAROLINE	**Мне всё равно.**	I don't care.
CLERK	**Они будут готовые в пятницу.**	They will be ready on Friday.

CAROLINE	Вы продаёте карты памяти?	Do you sell memory cards?
CLERK	Да. Что вам нужно?	Yes. What do you need?
CAROLINE	Карта памяти	A memory card
	(gigaBAYtaf) 16 гигабайтов.	sixteen gigabytes.
	И мне нужны две батерейки.	And I need two batteries.
CLERK	Вот вам, девушка.	Here you are, Miss.

Find the Russian words for the corresponding pictures in the word puzzle and then write them out in the spaces below.

   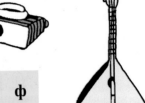

щ	ш	а	б	в	г	д	б	ф
м	а	т	р	ё	ш	к	а	э
д	р	ъ	ь	б	х	я	л	н
ш	к	а	т	у	л	к	а	з
я	е	т	б	ъ	и	ю	л	ь
ж	с	ц	з	г	х	щ	а	м
м	н	о	п	д	ы	ч	й	ё
б	а	т	а	р	е	й	к	а
щ	р	а	д	и	о	т	а	я

_____   _____

_____   _____

_____

(OPtik)
оптик
optician

(achKI)
очки
glasses

(aPRAva)
оправа
frame

(kanTAKTniye)   *(LINzy)*
контактные линзы
contact lenses

(OPtik)

ОПТИК

Optician

We hope that you will not need the following phrases, but better safe than sorry.

ТУРИСТ (Tourist)	*(pachiNIT)* *(achKI)* **Вы можете починить эти очки?**	Can you repair these glasses?
	(razBIL) *(stiKLO)* **Я разбил стекло и** *(aPRAvu)* **оправу.**	I've broken a lens and the frame.
ОПТИК	**Нет ли у вас запасных очков?**	Don't you have an extra pair?

ТУРИСТ	Да, есть. Но сломан *(SLOman)* заушник. *(zaUSHnik)*	Yes, I have. But the earpiece is broken.
ОПТИК	Легче найти новый заушник, чем вставить новое стекло.	It's easier to find a new earpiece, than put in a new lens.
ТУРИСТ	У меня есть контактные линзы, но я оставил их в гостинице.	I do have contact lenses, but I left them in the hotel.
ОПТИК	Ничего. У меня есть солнечные очки. *(SOLnichniye)* Среди них *(sriDI)* мы найдём заушник. *(nayDYOM)*	No problem. I have some sunglasses. Among them we'll find an earpiece.
ТУРИСТ	Спасибо большое. Не забудьте подвернуть винтик. *(zaBUfye)* *(padvirNUT)* *(VINtik)*	Thank you very much. Don't forget to tighten the screw.

РЕМОНТ ОБУВИ
(riMONT) *(Obuvi)*

Shoe repairs

(shnuROK)
шнурок
shoelace

(STYEL'ka)
стелька
insole

(Obuf')
обувь
shoes

All around town you are likely to see tiny shoeshine and shoe repair booths. Why not step inside and treat yourself to a shine? At the booths you can have minor repairs performed. For major repairs you can bring your shoes or boots to the shoe repair shops.

ТУРИСТКА (Tourist)	Почистите, пожалуйста. *(paCHIStitye)*	I'd like a shoeshine, please.
МАСТЕР (Repairman)	Вам нужны шнурки или *(shnurKI)* стельки?	Do you need any laces or insoles?

174

ТУРИСТКА	**Спасибо, но не надо.**	Thank you, but it's not necessary.
	Вы можете починить	Can you repair
	(sapaGI) **мои сапоги?**	my boots?
МАСТЕР	*(kabluKI)* **Только каблуки?**	Only the heels?
ТУРИСТКА	*(padMYOTki)* **И подмётки, если вы**	And the soles, too, if you
	можете сейчас.	can do it now.

Go over the material for the optician and shoe repair shops. Then see if you can fill in the blanks provided for the following emergency situations.

1. You have broken your eyeglasses. Ask if they can be repaired.

Вы можете ______________________________ **?**

2. Explain that you have broken a lens and the frame.

Я разбил ______________________________ **.**

3. Tell your friend that you left your contact lenses at the hotel.

Я оставил ______________________________ **в гостинице.**

4. You have broken your heel. Tell the shoemaker what you need.

Мне нужны новые ______________________________ **.**

5. An important business meeting is approaching. Can you get your shoes shined?

______________________________ .

ANSWERS

Fill in **1.** починить эти очки **2.** стекло и оправу **3.** контактные линзы **4.** каблуки **5.** Почистите, пожалуйста.

ESSENTIAL SERVICES

(bytaVIye)   *(uSLUgi)*
Бытовые услуги

25	*(BANK)* *(zbiriGAtil'naya)* *(KAsa)* # Банк / Сберегательная касса Bank Savings Bank	

(maNYEty)   *(bankNOty)*
МОНЕТЫ И БАНКНОТЫ
Coins and bills

Even after the fall of the Soviet Union in 1991, the basic unit of currency in Russia remained the **рубль** (ruble), which was divided into 100 **копейка** (kopecks). You can identify the old currency by the initials **CCCP** (USSR) and the hammer and sickle coat of arms.

In 1992 the **Банк России** (Bank of Russia) began issuing coins and banknotes. While there are still kopeck coins you may rarely see them, for in 2009 50 kopecks was worth only about 2 US cents.

As you repeat aloud the following denominations of bills and small change (**мелочь**), notice that the form of the word is determined by the number.

БАНКНОТЫ Bills/banknotes			
десять рублей	10 р.	пятьсот рублей	500 р.
пятьдесят рублей	50 р.	тысяча рублей	1000 р.
сто рублей	100 р.	пять тысяч рублей	5000 р.

МОНЕТЫ Coins			
одна копейка	1 к.	один рубль	1 р.
пять копеек	5 к.	два рубля	2 р.
десять копеек	10 к.	пять рублей	5 р.
пятьдесят копеек	50 к.	десять рублей	10 р.

(LYUdi)   *(VYEschi)*
Люди и вещи
People and things

(DYEN'gi)
деньги
money

(BANK)
банк
bank

(naLICHnye)
наличные
cash

(vaLYUta)
валюта
hard currency

(diRYEKtar)
директор
manager

(KAsa)
касса
teller's window

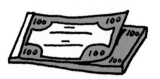

(daROZHniye) (CHEki)
дорожные чеки
travelers' checks

(SCHOT)
счёт
account

(zaYOM)
заём
loan

(priKHODny) (ORdir)
приходный ордер
deposit slip

(kriDITnaya) (KARtachka)
кредитная карточка
credit card

(rasKHODny) (ORdir)
расходный ордер
withdrawal slip

Как

How to

(abmiNYAT')
обменять
exchange

(abMYEny) (KURS)
обменный курс
rate of exchange

(plaTIT')
платить
pay

(atKRYT')   *(SCHOT)*
открыть счёт
open an account

(VYdaf)   *(FKLAT)*
выдать вклад
make a deposit

(priNYAT)   *(FKLAT)*
принять вклад
make a withdrawal

(raspiSAtsa)
расписаться
sign

(банкаMAT)
банкомат
Automatic Teller Machine

Mark and Caroline have to exchange dollars for rubles. They go the bank office at their hotel. Unfortunately, Mark has left his customs declaration form in his room.

MARK	*(abmiNYAT')* **Я хочу обменять**	I want to exchange some
	(DOlary) **американские доллары.**	American dollars.
КАССИРША (Teller)	**Сколько вы хотите обменять?**	How much do you want to exchange?
MARK	**Если можно, 100 долларов.**	If possible, 100 dollars.
КАССИРША	**Дайте мне ваш паспорт, пожалуйста.**	Give me your passport, please.

MARK	Я оставил паспорт в номере.	I left my passport in the room.
КАССИРША	*(nichiVO)* Без него я ничего не могу делать.	Without it I can do nothing.
CAROLINE	Вот мой паспорт, и я хочу обменять 500 долларов.	Here is my passport, and I wish to exchange 500 dollars.
КАССИРША	Всё вместе это будет 600 долларов.	All together that will be 600 dollars.
CAROLINE	Если можно, *(MYELkimi)* мелкими банкнотами.	If possible, small bills.
КАССИРША	Распишитесь, пожалуйста, вот здесь. *(kviTANtsiya)* Вот квитанция.	Please sign here. Here's a receipt.
	(dirZHYtye) Держите её.	Hold onto it.
MARK	Спасибо.	Thank you.
КАССИРША	*(SLYEduyuschi)* В следующий раз, не забудьте паспорт. Это важный документ.	Next time, please don't forget your passport. It's an important document.

Now look at the pictures and say the words aloud. Then write them in the blanks provided.

1. _____

2. _____

_____

3. _____

4. _____

6. _____

5. _____

(YA) (maGU)   *(YA) (khaCHU)*

Я могу / Я хочу

I can / I want

Do you remember the Russian verbs meaning "can" and "want"?

МОЧЬ	ХОТЕТЬ
can	want
я могу́	я хочу́
ты мо́жешь	ты хо́чешь
она мо́жет	он хо́чет
мы мо́жем	мы хоти́м
вы мо́жете	вы хоти́те
они мо́гут	они хотя́т

Now fill in the blanks of the following text with the correct forms of **мочь** and **хотеть**.

Марк _____ **обменять деньги в банке, но он не**
               wants

_____ **быть там в 10 часов утра. Его жена говорит, я тоже**
  able   be there   says

_____ **обменять дорожные чеки, и я** _____
  want   can

пойти в банк. Сколько долларов ты _____ **обменять? Марк**
go   want

отвечает, что я _____ **, и что я** _____ —
answers   want   can

это две разные вещи.
those are two different things

ANSWERS

Fill in хочет, может, хочу, могу, хочешь, хочу, могу

Fill in 5. расписаться 6. деньги

181

Most post offices — **Почта** — are open from 9 a.m. to 9 p.m. with an hour break for lunch. The **Главпочтамт** (main post office) also has **телеграф** (telegraph) and **телефон** (telephone) service and is open around the clock. Mailboxes are painted bright blue. You can purchase stamps at many newsstands and kiosks in addition to post office windows.

Read the following story about our amateur postman. Some of the words you will need are on the following pages.

Раиса говорит с Сашей, её маленьким сыном.

Raisa is speaking with Sasha, her little son.

— **Саша, что ты делаешь так рано?**

"Sasha, what are you doing so early?"

— **Я играю в почтальона.**
(pachtaLYON)

"I'm playing postman."

— **Какой ты почтальон? Где твои**
(PIS'ma)
письма?

"You are some mailman. Where are your letters?"

— **У меня есть письма, мама.**

"I have letters, Mom."

— **Откуда?**
(POMnish)

"Where from?"

— **Помнишь письма в твоём**
(shkaFU)
шкафу?

"Do you remember the letters in your closet?"

— **Те конверты с розовой лентой?**
(kanVYERty)

"Those envelopes with the pink ribbon?"

— **Да, мама. Я их раздавал**
(razdaVAL)
(saSYEdyam)
соседям.

"Yes, Mom. I gave them out to the neighbors."

— **Боже мой. Любовные письма**
от папы!

"My goodness. The love letters from Papa!"

(pachTOvy) *(YAschik)*
почтовый ящик
mailbox

(pachTOvaya buMAga)
почтовая бумага
writing paper

(MARki)
марки
stamps

(pis'MO)
письмо
letter

(atKRYTka)
открытка
postcard

(pachtaL'YON)
почтальон
mailman

Ваня и Надя идут на почту.

(paSYLka)
посылка
package

Steven discusses the post office with Nina.

STEVEN	*(atPRAvit')* **Я хочу отправить** *(aviapis'MO)* **авиаписьмо в США.**	I want to send an airmail letter to the USA.
NINA	**Я не знаю, сколько оно стоит. Пойдём на почту.**	I don't know how much it costs. Let's go to the post office.
STEVEN	*(paSLAT)* **Тогда я могу послать посылку сыну и дочке.**	Then I can send a package to my son and daughter.
NINA	*(sabiRAyut)* **Если они собирают марки, вы можете купить очень красивые наборы.**	If they collect stamps, you can purchase some very lovely sets.

STEVEN	Где можно послать _(tiliFAKS)_ телеграмму или телефакс?	Where can I send a telegram or fax?
NINA	Тоже на почте. Ещё что-нибудь?	Also at the post office. Anything else?
STEVEN	_(abiSCHAL)_ Я обещал позвонить _(naCHAL'niku)_ моему начальнику из России.	I promised to telephone my boss from Russia.
NINA	И это вы можете сделать на почте.	You can do that at the post office, too.
STEVEN	Всё ли можно сделать на почте?	Can you do everything at the post office?
NINA	Нет, не всё, но почти всё!	No, not everything, but almost everything!

На почте

At the post office

STEVEN	_(VAZHnaye)_ Я хочу отправить важное письмо в США.	I want to send an important letter to the USA.
СЛУЖАЩИЙ (Postal Clerk)	Можно послать авиапочтой _(zakazNYM)_ и заказным письмом.	It can be sent via airmail, and as a registered letter.
STEVEN	Мне нужно 3 марки по 15 р. и 10 марок по 25 р.	I need 3 stamps for 15 rubles and 10 stamps for 25 rubles.
СЛУЖАЩИЙ	Вам нужны конверты или открытки?	Do you need any envelopes or postcards?
STEVEN	Спасибо, но они у меня уже есть.	Thank you, but I already have them.

Конверт

The envelope

To address a Russian envelope you begin on the line **Куда** (where to) with the country, followed by the city, then the street address. On the line with **Кому** (to whom) write the person's last name followed by the initials for the first name and patronymic. The name goes in the **dative case**. Then provide your own address in the same order under the recipient's address.

Let's look at an example of an address:

Куда   _Россия_
Москва   117932
ул. Пушкина д.2 кв1
Кому _Ерофееву В.В._
От   _Россия_
Москва   117432
гостиница „Космос"
Смит Р.

THE DATIVE CASE

To send something to someone or call someone on the telephone, Russians place that person in the **dative case**. To form the **dative case** of masculine nouns, add **у** or **ю**. For most feminine nouns replace the **а** or **я** with **е**. With feminine nouns that end in **ия**, like **Мария**, the **dative** ending is **ии**. Feminine last names end in **ой**.

Иван → Ивану	**Юрий → Юрию**	**Пушкин → Пушкину**
Ирина → Ирине	**Катя → Кате**	**Вера → Вере**
Мариям → Марии	**Евгения → Евгении**	**Виктория → Виктории**
Иванова → Ивановой	**Каренина → Карениной**	**Толстая → Толстой**

You will want to review the dative case of the following pronouns:

мне to me	**тебе** to you	**ему** to him	**ей** to her
нам to us	**вам** to you	**им** to them	

Интернет

Personal computers and the internet have helped refine communication in the twenty-first century. The technology is changing so rapidly that one can hardly predict what the future holds. Most likely, however, we will still be reliant on small portable devices like laptops, digital music players, e-mail, and the world-wide web.

You can use these expressions to get help.

Помогите мне, пожалуйста, . . .	Help me, please, to . . .
читать электронную почту.	read my e-mail.
послать e-mail.*	send an e-mail.
напечатать страницу.	print a page.
найти веб-страницу.	find a web page.
сохранить файл.	save a file.
вводить тeхt.	enter text.
подключиться к сети интернет.	connect to the internet.
Мне нужен новый . . .	I need a new . . .
принтер.	printer.
сканер.	scanner.
монитор.	monitor.
нотбук.	laptop.
компьютер.	computer.
жёсткий диск.	hard disk.
Мне нужна новая . . .	I need a new . . .
клавиатура.	keyboard.
мышь.	mouse.

*Many words and expressions related to e-mail and the internet including the URLs or web addresses are typed with Roman characters. The suffix for Russia is **.ru** so you can experiment with sites like www.restoran.ru, www.teatr.ru, and even www.snowboarding.ru

Internet Sites

| Google | www.google.ru | Rambler | www.rambler.ru |
| Yahoo | www.yahoo.ru | Yandex | www.yandex.ru |

The Internet provides access to many useful sites, for travel and tourism, and for information in general. Some sites offer information in English as well as Russian. Look for the little British or American flag, or the indication **английский.** You might also add **/en** after the main address to see if an English version exists. Try reading the words aloud, or use an electronic translator and then compare the pages. Any list can only be a beginning, but there are some popular Russian search engines to find what you are looking for.

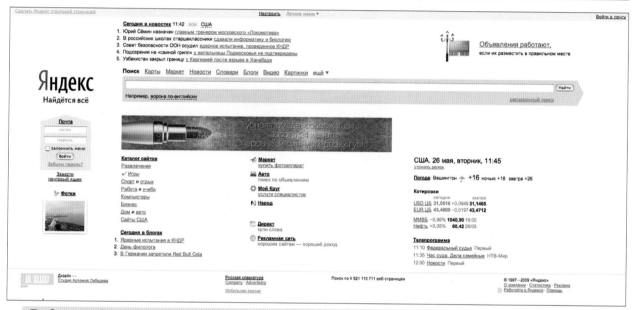

Before we leave the post office, write in the Russian words for the following important items in the spaces provided.

1. _____

2. _____

3. _____

4. _____

(aLYO) (aLYO) **АЛЛО! АЛЛО!**

Hello! Hello!

You can usually place local calls from your hotel room, either by dialing directly or by dialing a single number for an outside line. For international calls you may have to place an order through the international operator.

Here are some useful expressions for making telephone calls in Russia.

(MOZHna) (at) (VAS) (pazvaNIT')
Можно от вас позвонить?

Can I use your phone?

(kaKOY) (u)(VAS) (NOmir) (tiliFOna)
Какой у вас номер телефона?

What is your telephone number?

(YA) (khaCHU) (zakaZAT')
Я хочу   заказать _____ .

I want to order a _____ .

(VOT) (NOmir)
Вот номер.

Here is the number.

(I) (KOT) (GOrada)
И код города?

And the area code?

(mizhdugaRODny)   (razgaVOR)
междугородный разговор

long-distance call

(na) (chilaVYEka)
на человека

a person-to-person call

(mizhdunaRODny)   (razgaVOR)
международный разговор

international call

(na) (NOmir)
на номер

station-to-station

(DYEvushka) (nabiRAYtye) (paZHAlusta) (Etat) (NOmir)

Девушка, набирайте, пожалуйста, этот номер!

Operator, would you please dial this number for me!

(PLOkha) (SLYSHna)

Плохо слышно.

I can barely hear you.

(ZAnyata)

Занято.

The line is busy.

(MOZHna) (gavaRIT') (s)

Можно говорить с _____ ?

May I speak with _____ ?

(tiliFON) (aftaMAT)

телефон-автомат

pay telephone

(padniMAT) (TRUPku)

поднимать трубку

lift the receiver

(SOtavy) (tiliFON)

сотовый телефон

cell phone

(miNYA) (razyidiNIli)

Меня разъединили.

I've been disconnected.

(NYE) (klaDItye) (TRUPku)

Не кладите трубку!

Don't hang up!

(piriDAYtye) (yiMU) (paZHAlusta)

Передайте ему, пожалуйста.

Please give him a message.

(tiliFOnaya) (KNISHka)

телефонная книжка

telephone book

(nabiRAT') (NOmir)

набирать номер

dial a number

(maBIL'nik)

мобильник

mobile phone

THE INSTRUMENTAL CASE

When Russians speak with someone, they use the preposition **с** and the **instrumental case**. For masculine (and neuter) nouns, the **instrumental** ending is **ом (ем)** and **ым** in last names. For most feminine nouns the ending is **ой (ей)**.

Иван → с Иваном **Василий → с Василием** **Иванов → с Ивановым**

Анна → с Анной **Варя → с Варей** **Каренина → с Карениной**

You will also want to remember the following pronouns:

со мной with me **с тобой** with you **с ним** with him **с ней** with her

с нами with us **с вами** with you **с ними** with them

ТЕЛЕФОННАЯ КАБИНА

(tiliFOnaya)   *(kaBIna)*

Telephone booth

ТОМ	Да. (себе) Сперва я поднимаю *(padniMAyu)* трубку, потом опускаю монету. *(apuSKAyu)* Гудит. *(guDIT)* Хорошо! Я набираю *(nabiRAyu)* номер 234-09-58. Алло! Алло! Это говорит господин Буш.	Yes. (to himself) First I lift the receiver, then I drop the coin. It's ringing. That's good, I dial the number 234-09-58. Hello! Hello! This is Mr. Bush speaking.
ГОЛОС (A voice)	Плохо слышно. Говорите громче. *(GROmche)*	I can't hear you. Speak louder.
ТОМ	Попросите Бориса Николаевича *(papraSItye)* к телефону.	Please ask Boris Nikolaevich to come to the telephone.
ГОЛОС	Вы не туда попали.	You have the wrong number.
ТОМ	Извините за беспокойство. *(bispaKOYSTva)* (Он кладёт трубку и идёт обратно в гостиницу).	Excuse me for bothering you. (He puts down the receiver and goes back to his hotel.)

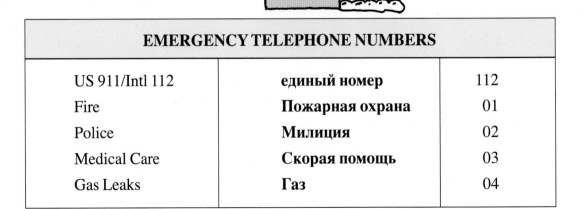

EMERGENCY TELEPHONE NUMBERS		
US 911/Intl 112	единый номер	112
Fire	Пожарная охрана	01
Police	Милиция	02
Medical Care	Скорая помощь	03
Gas Leaks	Газ	04

Here is a word search for you. Find the Russian equivalents for the following words, circle them,and then write them out for practice in the spaces below: **telephone, hello, receiver, dial, busy, number, area code, to call**.

а	б	в	т	е	л	е	ф	о	н
л	д	е	р	р	т	ы	и	п	а
л	щ	ч	у	г	з	ф	ь	ж	б
о	з	х	б	ц	а	б	н	м	и
а	с	ф	к	д	н	о	м	е	р
я	ч	ы	а	ш	я	ф	г	у	а
к	о	д	и	ё	т	ю	ъ	щ	т
ф	п	о	з	в	о	н	и	т	ь

ANSWERS

Word search телефон, алло, трубка, набирать, занято, номер, код, позвонить

(paftaRYEniye)　　　　　　(MAT)　　(uCHEniya)
ПОВТОРЕНИЕ МАТЬ УЧЕНИЯ

Repetition is the mother of learning

Нина and **Александр** are studying the parts of the body. See if you can learn the words along with them.

НИНА	(nachiNAit) **Ну, кто начинает —** **ты или я?**	Well, who should begin — you or I?
АЛЕКСАНДР	(SPRAshivat') **Ты начинаешь спрашивать,** (atviCHAT') **и я буду отвечать на** **вопросы.**	You begin the questioning, and I'll answer the questions.
НИНА	**Хорошо, что у тебя** **вот здесь?**	Okay, what do you have right here?
АЛЕКСАНДР	(VOlasy) **Волосы.**	Hair.
НИНА	**А что это?**	And what is this?
АЛЕКСАНДР	(GLAS) **Один глаз, но у тебя** (GLAza) **два глаза.**	One eye, but you have two eyes.
НИНА	**А между глазами?**	And between the eyes?
АЛЕКСАНДР	(NOS) **Это мой нос.**	That's my nose.

НИНА	**Это твой *(ROT)* рот, а что это над ртом? *(RTOM)***	 This is your mouth, but what is above the mouth?
АЛЕКСАНДР	**Ты имеешь ввиду усы? *(uSY)***	 Do you mean my moustache?
НИНА	**Да. У тебя одно ухо? *(Ukha)***	 Yes. Do you have one ear?
АЛЕКСАНДР	**Нет, два глаза, и два уха.**	No, two eyes, and two ears.
НИНА	**А это моя щека. *(schiKA)***	 And this is my cheek.
АЛЕКСАНДР	**А это твоё лицо, *(liTSO)***	 And this is your face,
	и твоя голова. *(galaVA)*	 and your head.
НИНА	**Когда ты улыбаешься, я вижу . . .**	When you smile, I see . . .
АЛЕКСАНДР	**Мои зубы. У врача я показываю . . .**	 My teeth. At the doctor's I Put out my . . .
НИНА	**Язык. *(yiZYK)***	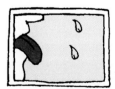 Tongue.
	Это подбородок. *(padbaROdak)*	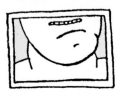 This is a chin.

АЛЕКСАНДР	А это, конечно, *(SHEya)* **шея.**	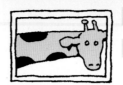	And this is, of course, the neck.
НИНА	*(pliCHO)* **Вот одно плечо,**		Here is one shoulder,
АЛЕКСАНДР	**Плюс моё плечо,** *(pliCHA)* **два плеча.**		Plus my shoulder, is two shoulders.
НИНА	*(ruKA)* *(ruKI)* **Одна рука, а две руки . . .**		One arm, two arms . . .
АЛЕКСАНДР	**Но мы говорим «все руки».**		But we say "all the arms."
НИНА	*(LOkat')* *(LOKtya)* **Один локоть или два локтя.**		One elbow or two elbows.
АЛЕКСАНДР	**Мы говорим «все наши локти».**		We say "all our elbows."
НИНА	*(PAL'tsif)* *(ruKYE)* **Сколько пальцев на руке?**		How many fingers on a hand?
АЛЕКСАНДР	*(PAlits)* *(PAL'tsa)* **Один палец, два пальца, три пальца,четыре пальца, пять пальцев.**		One finger, two fingers, three fingers, four fingers, five fingers.
НИНА	**А у меня и десять пальцев.**		And I have ten fingers, too.
АЛЕКСАНДР	**Да, но не все пальцы на одной руке!**		Yes, but not all ten fingers on one hand!
НИНА	**Как всегда, ты прав.**		As always, you're right.
АЛЕКСАНДР	*(zadaYU)* **Теперь я задаю вопросы. Это**		Now I'll ask the questions. This is the
НИНА	*(spiNA)* **спина.**		back.
АЛЕКСАНДР	**Впереди находится**		In front is the
НИНА	*(GRUT')* **грудь.**		breast.
АЛЕКСАНДР	**Когда ты слишком много** *(YESH)* *(baLIT)* **ешь, что у тебя болит?**		When you eat too much, what hurts?
НИНА	*(zhiLUdak)* **Желудок.**		My stomach.
АЛЕКСАНДР	**Правильно. А ещё ниже мы находим**		That's correct. And even lower we find

НИНА	*(zhiVOT)* **живот.**	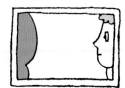	the belly.
АЛЕКСАНДР	**А сзади**		And in the back is the
НИНА	*(ZADnitsa)* **задница.**		backside.

АЛЕКСАНДР	*(kaLYEna)* **У тебя одно колено?**		And do you have one knee?
НИНА	**Нет, два колена.**		No, two knees.

АЛЕКСАНДР	*(naGA)* **И не одна нога, а** *(naGI)* **две ноги.**		And not a single leg, but two legs.

НИНА	*(naGYE)* **И на каждой ноге** *(staPA)* *(PYATka)* **стопа, пятка, и**		And each foot has a sole, heel, and
АЛЕКСАНДР	**пять пальцев ноги.**		five toes.

That was certainly a lot of new words to learn. Try repeating them to yourself several times and then see if you can draw lines matching the Russian words with their English equivalents.

1.	голова	**а.**	leg/foot
2.	рот	**б.**	ear
3.	нога	**в.**	elbow
4.	рука	**г.**	finger
5.	плечо	**д.**	arm/hand
6.	живот	**е.**	head
7.	колено	**ж.**	mouth
8.	локоть	**з.**	knee
9.	палец	**и.**	shoulder
10.	ухо	**к.**	belly

ANSWERS

Matching 1.е 2.ж 3.а 4.д 5.и 6.к 7.з 8.в 9.г 10.б

195

(LYOkaye)
лёгкое
lung

(PYEchin')
печень
liver

(MYSHtsa)
мышца
muscle

(arTYEriya)
артерия
artery

(VYEna)
вена
vein

(SERtse)
сердце
heart

(zhiLUdak)
желудок
stomach

(kiSHECHnik)
кишечник
intestines

(POCHka)
почка
kidney

(SHTO)   (u) (VAS)   (baLIT)

Что у вас болит?
What hurts?

To say in Russian that you are ill or something hurts, you need the expression **у меня, у вас**, etc. Literally, this means I have, you have [something that aches]. We use the genitive case of the pronouns after the preposition **у**.

у кого — who has

у меня — I have	**у нас** — we have
у тебя — you have	**у вас** — you have
у него — he has	**у них** — they have
у неё — she has	

We hope you won't need to use them, but the following expressions for basic aches and pains are good ones to learn, **на всякий случай** (just in case). In an emergency you will want to call the number for immediate care — **Скорая помощь**. The emergency phone number in most of Europe is **112**. When you identify yourself as a foreigner and describe the problem, a physician will be at your hotel within minutes to see you. In non-emergency situations you should call your embassy or ask your hosts or the hotel personnel for the location of the nearest polyclinic.

(u) *(vraCHA)*

У ВРАЧА

At the doctor's

If you become ill on your trip, the following list of expressions will come in handy to communicate with the doctor.

Я чувствую себя плохо.		I don't feel well.
Я заболел.		I feel sick.
У меня высокая температура.		I have a high temperature.
Болит здесь.		It hurts here.
У меня болит _____ .		My _____ hurts.
голова		head
бедро		hip
горло		throat
ребро		rib
У меня _____ .		I have _____ .
перелом		a broken bone
ушиб		a bruise
ожог		a burn
насморк		a head cold
кашель		a cough
понос		diarrhea
запор		constipation
температура		a fever
Откройте рот!		Open your mouth!
Покажите язык!		Stick out your tongue!
Разденьтесь (до пояса)!		Undress (to the waist)!
Ложитесь!		Lie down!

Вы мне выпишете лекарство?		Are you going to give me a prescription?
Как часто принимать лекарство?		How often should I take the medicine?

(zubNOY) *(VRACH)* *(atKROYtye)* *(ROT)*
ЗУБНОЙ ВРАЧ: ОТКРОЙТЕ РОТ!
The dentist: Open your mouth!

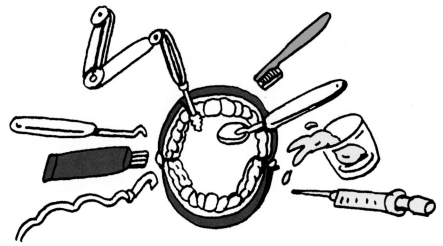

It hasn't been a happy day for Stefanie who goes to visit the dentist with a toothache.

STEFANIE	**У меня страшно болит зуб.**	I have a terrible toothache.
ЗУБНОЙ ВРАЧ	*(PLOMbu)* **Вы потеряли пломбу.**	You've lost a filling.
STEFANIE	**Можете поставить новую пломбу?**	Can you put in a new filling?
ЗУБНОЙ ВРАЧ	*(inFYEKtsii)* **Да, если нет инфекции.**	Yes, if there's no infection.
STEFANIE	*(amal'GAmu)* **Вы поставите амальгаму?**	Will you put in an amalgam filling?
ЗУБНОЙ ВРАЧ	*(VRYEminuyu)* **Нет, только временную.** **Когда вы вернётесь домой, обратитесь к вашему зубному врачу.**	No, just a temporary one. When you return home, go to your own dentist.
STEFANIE	**Спасибо. Кстати, сколько стоит новая** *(kaRONka)* **коронка?**	Thank you. By the way, how much does a new crown cost?
ЗУБНОЙ ВРАЧ	**Не думайте об этом!**	Don't even think about that!
STEFANIE	**А не надо удалить этот зуб?**	And you don't have to pull this tooth?

198

ЗУБНОЙ ВРАЧ STEFANIE	**Нет, всё в порядке.** **Хорошо! Всего** **доброго.**	No, everything is in order. Okay! Have a nice day.

(v)   (bal'NItse)

В БОЛЬНИЦЕ

At the hospital

Now read along as Mark describes his visit to a Russian hospital.

Сегодня утром я вдруг почувствовал	This morning I suddenly felt ill.
себя плохо. Вызвали врача, который	They summoned a doctor, who
осмотрел меня, и потом	examined me and then
посоветовал мне лечь в больницу.	recommended that I go to a hospital.
В больнице медсестра измерила	At the hospital a nurse measured
моё давление и температуру.	my blood pressure and temperature.
Потом сделали анализ крови.	Then they did a blood analysis.
Врач слушал пульс, сердце и	The doctor listened to my pulse, heart
лёгкие. Он решил не делать	and lungs. He decided not to perform an
операцию, а сделал укол,	operation, but gave me a shot,
и выписал рецепт на	and wrote out a prescription for
лекарство.	some medicine.

Have fun with the crossword puzzle using expressions you've learned and might need in a medical emergency. We've given you a start with the word for "patient" — **больной**.

Кроссворд

по горизонтали
ACROSS

4. nurse
5. prescription
7. patient
9. tooth
10. eye

по вертикали
DOWN

1. temperature
2. nose
3. doctor
6. pulse
8. mouth

200

(KRAYnyaya)   *(niabkhaDImast')*

КРАЙНЯЯ НЕОБХОДИМОСТЬ

An emergency

Russia has traditionally been a safe country for tourists. While most people are honest, friendly and helpful, hard economic times have given rise to more street crime.

We hope you don't find yourself in a medical or other emergency situation, but it is a good idea to know some useful words and phrases.

First, here are the vital phone numbers:

(miLItsiya)
Милиция   02
Police

(SKOraya) (POmasch)
Скорая помощь   03
Emergency First Aid

(yiDIny)   *(NOmir)*
Единый номер   112
Unified emergency number

(maSHYna)

МАШИНА СКОРОЙ ПОМОЩИ И

(midiTSYNskaya)   *(POmasch)*

МЕДИЦИНСКАЯ ПОМОЩЬ

Ambulance and medical help

To get emergency medical aid from your hotel notify the front desk staff. They can call for an ambulance with trained medical personnel to assist you on the spot or to transport you to the hospital. Here are a few expressions for you to learn.

машина скорой помощи ambulance	**крайняя необходимость** emergency	**больница** hospital

(pamaGItye)
Помогите!   Help!

(VYzavitye)   (vraCHA)
Вызовите врача!   Call for a doctor!

Вызовите скорую помощь!   Call an ambulance!

Отвезите меня в больницу!   Take me to a hospital!

(uPAL)
Я упал.   I fell.

(SBIla)
Меня сбила машина.   I was hit by a car.

(sirDYECHny)   (PRIstup)
У меня сердечный приступ.   I'm having a heart attack.

Я обварился.   I burned myself.

Я порезалась.   I cut myself.

(kravatiCHEniye)
У меня кровотечение.   I'm bleeding.

(patiRYAla)   (KROvi)
Я потеряла много крови.   I've lost a lot of blood.

(piriLOM)
Я думаю, у меня перелом.   I think the bone is broken.

Нога вздута.   The leg is swollen.

Запястье растянуто.   The wrist is twisted.

(laDYSHKa)   (VYvykhnuta)
Лодыжка вывихнута.   My ankle is dislocated.

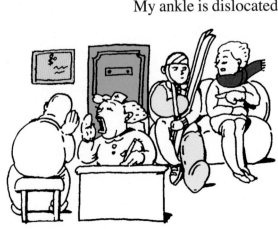

(miLItsiya)

МИЛИЦИЯ

The police (militia)

(miLItsianir)
милиционер

policeman

(miliTSEYski)   *(uCHAStak)*
милицейский   **участок**

police (militia) station

In most Russian cities you can find police officers directing traffic and patroling the streets. If you have problems, the police can probably help you — from finding your way to finding lost items. Items that you have lost often turn up. If you do leave something in a restaurant, museum or hotel, don't assume it's gone forever. Check first with the local staff, or with the police. You might want to ask for the Lost and Found Bureau (**Бюро находок**).

Here are some expressions you should know in case you need to call the police.

(miLItsiyu)
Вызовите милицию!   Call the police!

(bliZHAYschi)
Где ближайший   Where is the nearest

милицейский участок?   police station?

(patiRYAla)
Я потеряла мой паспорт.   I've lost my passport.

Я потерялся.   I'm lost.

(uKRAli)   *(buMAZHnik)*
Украли мой бумажник.   My wallet has been stolen.

203

BEFORE YOU LEAVE

(da) (atYEZda)

До отъезда

You've learned a lot of Russian by now — probably much more than you realize. This section is a very important step in the learning process — a step in which you can review and solidify your understanding of the new language.

We've organized the section around basic situations you might encounter. For each situation there are a number of questions about appropriate Russian expressions. If you have difficulty remembering what to say in a particular situation, review the relevant unit in this book.

Good luck and have a good trip!

Счастливого пути!

Situation 1: Давайте познакомимся!
Let's get acquainted!

1. When you meet a Russian, how do you start up a conversation?
   a. **Хорошо, спасибо.**
   б. **Не волнуйтесь.**
   в. **Здравствуйте.**

2. You hear the question **«Как вас зовут?»** You should reply:
   a. **До свидания.**
   б. **Меня зовут** ——————.
   в. **Я из США.**

3. Someone asks how are things (**«Как дела?»**). How should you reply?
   a. **Хорошо, спасибо.**
   б. **Вы правы.**
   в. **Что нам делать?**

4. If someone does you a favor, you might want to say "thank you."
   a. **Вот моя жена.**
   б. **Спасибо.**
   в. **Здравствуйте.**

5. When you part, you say "goodbye" to your new acquaintance.
   a. **Как вам помочь?**
   б. **Извините, пожалуйста.**
   в. **До свидания.**

Situation 2: Приезд
Arrival

1. To reserve a hotel room you tell the room clerk:
   а. **Идите прямо.**
   б. **Я хочу забронировать номер.**
   в. **Окно не открывается.**

2. If you need a room with a shower you ask for:
   а. **номер с душем.**
   б. **ключ в номер.**
   в. **завтрак в буфете.**

3. What do you want to say if the television doesn't work?
   а. **Погода неплохая.**
   б. **Телевизор не работает.**
   в. **Туалет не работает.**

4. How do you find where the snack bar is located?
   а. **Вы не скажете, где здесь буфет?**
   б. **Как насчёт завтрака?**
   в. **А где лифт?**

Situation 3: Достопримечательности
Places of interest

1. Suggest to your companion that you go by subway.
   а. **Поедем на такси.**
   б. **Давайте поедем на автобусе.**
   в. **Поедем на метро.**

2. Can you tell your next appointment that you'll be there at 11 o'clock?
   а. **Я приду в одиннадцать часов.**
   б. **Билет стоит десять рублей.**
   в. **Шестой этаж.**

3. Please communicate to the clerk that you are working on Saturday.

   а. Я иду в пятницу.
   б. Иван завтракает в семь часов.
   в. Я работаю в субботу.

4. Can you ask the price of a ticket to **Новгород**?

   а. Сколько стоит билет в Новгород?
   б. Нам нужно два купе?
   в. Когда отправляется поезд в Санкт-Петербург?

5. Try to tell your hosts that you are an American, but you understand Russian.

   а. Я армянин, но говорю по-английски.
   б. Я американка, но я понимаю по-русски.
   в. Я украинка, но читаю по-русски.

6. Which of the following persons is likely to have difficulty getting around?

   а. Мария живёт в Англии, и она хорошо говорит по-английски.
   б. Роберт работает в Москве, но не понимает по-русски.
   в. Ваня поедет в Токио, и он понимает по-японски.

7. What do you need to know to rent a small car?

   а. Я хотел бы взять напрокат маленькую машину.
   б. Мне нужен микроавтобус.
   в. Можно купить большую машину у вас?

8. At the service station you ask the attendant to check the water and oil.

   а. Как проехать в Кремль?
   б. У вас есть автодорожная карта?
   в. Проверьте, пожалуйста, воду и масло.

9. Can you choose the most unlikely weather report?

   а. В Москве в феврале идёт снег.
   б. В Санкт-Петербурге в июне хорошая погода.
   в. В Одессе в августе очень холодно.

10. What can you assume when your guide tells you «Сегодня пятница.»

    а. Вчера был четверг.
    б. Завтра будет понедельник.
    в. Завтра будет среда.

11. Where must you go when you arrive at the **Аэропорт**?

    а. Вокзал.
    б. Паспортный контроль.
    в. Сентябрь.

12. How would you ask the length of the flight?

   а. Сколько времени длится наш полёт?
   б. Где наши места?
   в. Когда вы будете нас кормить?

Situation 4: Развлечение

Entertainment

1. Can you invite your business acquaintance to the ballet this evening?

   а. Хотите пойти в кинотеатр сегодня?
   б. У меня два билета на оперу завтра.
   в. Хотите пойти в Большой театр на балет сегодня вечером?

2. Tell the hotel clerk that you like to jog in the morning.

   а. Моя жена плавает каждый вечер.
   б. Я бегаю каждое утро.
   в. Я смотрю футбол и баскетбол по телевизору.

Situation 5: Заказать обед

Ordering a meal

1. Find out what's for breakfast.

   а. Где мы будем обедать?
   б. Что сегодня на завтрак?
   в. Вам нравится суп?

2. Tell the waiter that you'll take the fish course.

   а. Мы предпочитаем салат.
   б. Они ужинают вечером.
   в. Я возьму рыбу.

3. Ask for a copy of the menu to look at.

   а. Принесите, пожалуйста, меню.
   б. Я сейчас принесу закуски.
   в. Вы любите икру?

ANSWERS

Situation 3 12. а   Situation 4 1. в 2. б   Situation 5 1. б 2. в 3. а

4. Ask the waitress for her suggestions.
   а. Что вы нам советуете?
   б. Я возьму русский салат.
   в. Принесите, пожалуйста, борщ.

5. What dish might you choose for an appetizer?
   а. Соль и перец.
   б. Чай с сахаром.
   в. Ассорти мясное.

6. Choose a main course.
   а. На сладкое я люблю мороженое.
   б. На второе я возьму сёмгу.
   в. Принесите, пожалуйста, бутылку шампанского.

7. You forgot to ask for some famous Russian black bread.
   а. И чёрный хлеб и масло.
   б. И кофе и пирожное.
   в. Нам красное вино, пожалуйста.

8. Try to find out what's for dessert.
   а. Что мы будем пить?
   б. Что на сладкое?
   в. Я сейчас принесу салфетку.

Situation 6: В магазине

At the store

1. You've made your way to the store with the sign **ОДЕЖДА**. What items will you **not** find there?
   а. носки, рубашки, свитер
   б. платье, юбка, блузка
   в. бритва, лезвия, духи

2. Ask the salesperson if your companion can try on the suit.
   а. Можно примерить костюм?
   б. Покажите нам, пожалуйста, сапоги.
   в. Сколько стоит этот модный галстук?

3. Now you're off to the **ГАСТРОНОМ**. Which list will you need for your shopping?
   a. зубная щётка, расчёска, зеркало
   б. ботинки, шляпа, перчатки
   в. молоко, овощи, фрукты, мясо

4. You're still at the **ГАСТРОНОМ**. Which item won't you find there?
   a. десять литров бензина
   б. банка кофе
   в. десяток яиц

5. Which of the following do you still need to purchase at the **РЫНОК**?
   a. телевизор и радио
   б. юбка и блузка
   в. рыба и мороженое

6. At the big department store you see **Отдел ПАРФЮМЕРИЯ**. What might you purchase there?
   a. Дайте мне, пожалуйста, десяток яиц и пачку сахара.
   б. Я возьму кусок мыла, шампунь и лак для волос.
   в. Покажите мне, пожалуйста, коробку конфет.

7. Oh! Oh! You've come down with a headache. Quick! Off to the **АПТЕКА**.
   a. У вас есть что-нибудь от зубной боли?
   б. Я возьму глазные капли.
   в. Мне нужен аспирин.

8. You ask the **Горничная** to do your laundry and iron your shirts.
   a. Пришейте, пожалуйста, пуговицу.
   б. Вы можете постирать бельё и погладить рубашки?
   в. Это не мои носки, один красный, другой зелёный.

9. Before you do any more shopping you sit down for a quick haircut. What do you **not** want to have done at the **Парикмахерская**?
   a. Я хочу постричься.
   б. Вымойте мне голову.
   в. Вы можете мой костюм сдать в чистку?

Match up your needs with the shops and stores.

1. Мы хотим купить русский самовар.
2. Я люблю слушать классическую музыку.
3. Вы печатаете с карты памяти?
4. Мне нужны подмётки и каблуки.
5. Я сегодня купил блокнот и конверты.
6. Вы можете починить эти очки?
7. Мне надо купить жене кольцо или серьги.
8. Где можно купить газеты и журналы?
9. Мои часы спешат. Что делать?
10. Сделайте мне стрижку и укладку.

а. Женский зал
б. Газетный киоск
в. Канцелярские товары
г. Ювелирные изделия
д. Ремонт часов
е. Подарки
ж. Фототовары
з. Ремонт обуви
и. Ремонт очков
к. Музыка

Situation 7: Бытовые услуги

Essential services

1. You need some more money for souvenir shopping. You go to the **БАНК**.
   а. **Я хочу обменять сто долларов.**
   б. **Вы продаёте марки?**
   в. **Извините. Вы не знаете, где почта?**

2. Can you find out today's exchange rate?
   а. **Можно открыть счёт?**
   б. **Какой сегодня обменный курс?**
   в. **Можно платить кредитной карточкой?**

3. Let's drop into the local **ПОЧТА** and send a fax back home.
   а. **Мы хотим послать телефакс. Вы можете нам помочь?**
   б. **Сколько стоит эта открытка?**
   в. **Я хочу отправить письмо в США.**

4. Ask your new friend for his telephone number in **Москва**.
   а. **Я хочу заказать международный разговор.**
   б. **Можно от вас позвонить?**
   в. **Какой у вас номер телефона?**

5. You've just dialed the emergency number.
   What do you hope to hear?
   а. **Погода плохая!**
   б. **Скорая помощь!**
   в. **Извините за беспокойство!**

6. Tell the doctor that your throat hurts.
   а. **У меня болит горло.**
   б. **У меня понос.**
   в. **Разденьтесь!**

7. Which of the following would you probably not hear at the dentist's?

    а. Он поставит пломбу.

    б. Мы сделаем анализ крови.

    в. Сколько стоит новая коронка?

8. When you were at the hospital, what service was not provided?

    а. Выписали рецепт на лекарство.

    б. Принесли водку и икру.

    в. Сделали операцию.

9. If you run into trouble, how will you ask for help?

    а. Помогите!

    б. Читайте!

    в. Ложитесь!

10. The nicest words in Russian for your hosts to hear is a polite "thank you" — **по-русски**.

    а. Двадцать рублей.

    б. У меня маленькая проблема.

    в. Спасибо большое.

ANSWERS

Situation 7   7.б 8.б 9.а 10.в

numbers 1–10

one	six
two	seven
three	eight
four	nine
five	ten

days of the week

Monday	Friday
Tuesday	Saturday
Wednesday	Sunday
Thursday	

months

January	July
February	August
March	September
April	October
May	November
June	December

numbers 11–20

eleven	sixteen
twelve	seventeen
thirteen	eighteen
fourteen	nineteen
fifteen	twenty

seasons of the year

spring	fall
summer	winter

in the morning	in the evening
during the day	at night

numbers 21–101

twenty-one	seventy
thirty	eighty
forty	ninety
fifty	one hundred
sixty	one hundred one

to ride/drive (to go by vehicle)

I am going	we are going
you are going	you are going
she/he is going	they are going

to go/walk

I am going	we are going
you are going	you are going
he/she is going	they are going

ме́сяцы

янва́рь	ию́ль
февра́ль	а́вгуст
март	сентя́брь
апре́ль	октя́брь
май	ноя́брь
ию́нь	дека́брь

дни неде́ли

понеде́льник	пя́тница
вто́рник	суббо́та
среда́	воскресе́нье
четве́рг	

числа
1–10

оди́н	шесть
два	семь
три	во́семь
четы́ре	де́вять
пять	де́сять

у́тром	ве́чером
днём	но́чью

времена́ го́да

весна́	о́сень
ле́то	зима́

числа
11–20

оди́ннадцать	шестна́дцать
двена́дцать	семна́дцать
трина́дцать	восемна́дцать
четы́рнадцать	девятна́дцать
пятна́дцать	два́дцать

идти́

я иду́	мы идём
ты идёшь	вы идёте
он/она́ идёт	они́ иду́т

е́хать

я е́ду	мы е́дем
ты е́дешь	вы е́дете
она́/он е́дет	они́ е́дут

числа
21–101

два́дцать оди́н	се́мьдесят
три́дцать	во́семьдесят
со́рок	девяно́сто
пятьдеся́т	сто
шестьдеся́т	сто оди́н

Hello.	**Please.**	**What is your name?**
	Thank you.	
	You're welcome.	My name is . . .
Goodbye.	**Excuse me.**	
Russia	**America** **U.S.A.**	**Canada**
I am a Russian. (m)		I am Canadian. (m)
	I am an American. (f)	
I am a Russian. (f)		
	I am an American. (m)	I am Canadian. (f)
England	**to speak**	**to understand**
		Do you understand English?
I am an Englishwoman.	I (don't) speak Russian.	
		I (don't) understand Russian.
I am an Englishman.	Do you speak English?	

Как вас зовут?

Меня зовут . . .

Пожа́луйста.

Спаси́бо.

Пожа́луйста.

Извини́те.

Здра́вствуйте.

До свида́ния.

Кана́да

Я кана́дец.

Я кана́дка.

Аме́рика
С Ш А

Я америка́нка.

Я америка́нец.

Росси́я

Я ру́сский.

Я ру́сская.

понима́ть

Вы понима́ете по-англи́йски?

Я (не) понима́ю по-ру́сски.

говори́ть

Я (не) говорю́ по-русски.

Вы говори́те по-англи́йски?

А́нглия

Я англича́нка.

Я ангича́нин.

uncle aunt

sister brother

my family

grandmother grandfather
mother father
daughter son

questions

Who? How?
What? When?
Where? Where to?
How much/many?

What do you need?

I need . . .

What do you want?

I want

to see.

to buy.

Please tell me!

Please show me!

Please give me!

Whose is it?

mine (my) our(s)
your(s) your(s)
his, her(s) their(s)

Who is this?

I we
you you
he/she/it they

Can you?

Yes, I can.

No, I can't.

вопросы

Кто?	Как?
Что?	Когда?
Где?	Куда?
Ско́лько?	

моя семья

ба́бушка	де́душка
мать	оте́ц
дочь	сын

дя́дя	тётя
сестра́	брат

Скажи́те, пожа́луйста.

Покажи́те, пожа́луйста.

Да́йте, пожа́луйста.

Что вы хоти́те?

Я хочу́

посмотре́ть.

купи́ть.

Что вам ну́жно?

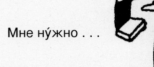

Мне ну́жно . . .

Вы мо́жете?

Да, я могу́.

Нет, я не могу́.

Кто э́то?

я	мы
ты	вы
он/она́/оно́	они́

Чей э́то?

мой, моя́	наш, на́ша
моё, мои́	на́ше, на́ши
твой, твоя́	ваш, ва́ша
твоё, твои́	ва́ше, ва́ши
его́, её	их

in the taxi

Are you available?
I (have to go) to the hotel Kosmos.
How much do I owe you?

on the metro

How do I get to the Kremlin?
How many stops to the theater?
How much does the trip cost?

at the hotel

Where is the key?
Where is the elevator?
I need another towel.
The shower doesn't work;
       nor does the lamp.

directions

to the left   forward   to the right
      backwards

on a train

Where are our seats?
Car 10, seats 7 and 8.
When does the train depart?

When?

At one.	At five.
At two.	At ten.
At three.	At twelve.
At four.	At thirteen (1:00 PM).

at the airport

Where is our luggage?
When do we take off?
When will we land?

What kind of weather?

Today it's . . .   cold.
        warm.
        hot.
Is it raining or snowing?

the car

Please check the . . .   oil.
        tires.
        brakes.

в гости́нице

Где ключ?
Где лифт?
Мне ну́жно ещё полоте́нце.
Душ не рабо́тает;
    ла́мпа не рабо́тает.

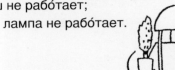

на метро́

Как прое́хать в Кремль?
Ско́лько остано́вок до теа́тра?
Ско́лько сто́ит прое́зд?

на такси́

Вы свобо́дны?
Мне в гости́ницу Ко́смос.
Ско́лько с меня́?

Когда́?

В час.
В два часа́.
В три часа́.
В четы́ре часа́.

В пять часо́в.
В де́сять часо́в.
В двена́дцать часо́в.
В трина́дцать часо́в.

на по́езд

Где на́ши места́?
Ваго́н 10, места́ 7 и 8.
Когда́ отправля́ется по́езд?

направле́ние движе́ния

вперёд

нале́во ← → напра́во

наза́д

маши́на

Прове́рьте, пожа́луйста . . .
    ма́сло.
    ши́ны.
    тормоза́.

Кака́я пого́да?

Сего́дня . . .
    хо́лодно.
    тепло́.
    жа́рко.

Идёт дождь и́ли снег?

в аэропо́рту

Где наш бага́ж?
Когда́ вы́лет?
Когда́ мы приземли́мся?

How?

so pretty
very tasty
too expensive

What is that?

a good pharmacy
a poor snack bar
an interesting place
old books

What kind of people?

a big boy
a little girl

young people

The Bolshoi Theater

One ticket to the ballet?
Two tickets to the opera. Row 5,
    seats 7 and 8.
Opera glasses for me, please.

You

Do you have a city map?	genitive
I will telephone you.	dative
What's your name?	accusative
Who is with you?	instrumental
We know about you.	prepositional

I

I have some money.	genitive
Give it to me.	dative
My name is Oleg.	accusative
Will you go with me?	instrumental
What did you say about me?	prepositional

What's for breakfast?

juice   cheese   butter
bread   jelly
     tea with sugar
     coffee without milk

What do you like?
     I like everything.

What do you love to do?
     I love to play cards.

sport(s)

Who jogs?
I swim.
Papa watches soccer.
Mama rests and sunbathes.

Что за лю́ди?

большо́й ма́льчик
ма́ленькая де́вочка

молоды́е лю́ди

Что э́то?

хоро́шая апте́ка
плохо́й буфе́т
интере́сное ме́сто
ста́рые кни́ги

Как?

так краси́во
о́чень вку́сно
сли́шком до́рого

Я

У меня́ есть де́ньги.

Да́йте мне.

Меня́ зову́т Оле́г.

Вы пойдёте со мной?

Что вы сказа́ли обо мне?

Вы

У вас есть план го́рода?
Я вам позвоню́
Как вас зову́т.
Кто с ва́ми?
Мы зна́ем о вас.

Большо́й теа́тр!

Оди́н биле́т на бале́т?
Два биле́та на о́перу. Ряд 5,
    места́ 7 и 8.
Мне бино́кль, пожа́луйста.

спорт

Кто бе́гает?
Я пла́ваю.
Па́па смо́трит футбо́л.
Ма́ма отдыха́хет и загора́ет.

Что вам нра́вится?

Мне нра́вится всё.

Что вы лю́бите делать?

Я люблю́ игра́ть в карты.

Что на за́втрак?

сок   сыр   ма́сло
хлеб   варенье
    чай с са́харом
    ко́фе без молока́

the restaurant

menu   waiter
first course   second course   third course
              beverages
              Bon appetit!

supper at the buffet

a sandwich   with caviar
                        with cheese

I'll take
                        soda.
          a glass of
                        champagne.

What's for dinner?

soup   salad
fish   or   meat
wine   or   beer

shops

Supermarket   Bakery
Vegetables   Fruits
Pastries   Ice Cream

women's clothing

blouse   skirt
dress   shawl
bra   slip
panties   panty hose

men's clothing

shirt   slacks
suit   tie
underpants   socks
undershirt

pharmacy

        I need something for
a cough   constipation   diarrhea

        Do you have
antacid   aspirin   bandages

toiletries

toothbrush   toothpaste
comb   tissues
soap   shampoo

the market

How much does it weigh?
How much does it cost?

I'll take 100 grams.
Give me half a kilo (about a pound).

Что на обе́д?

суп		сала́т
ры́ба	или	мя́со
вино́	или	пи́во

ужин в буфе́те

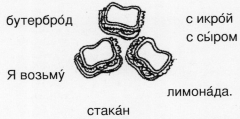

бутербро́д   с икро́й
с сы́ром

Я возьму́

лимона́да.

стака́н

шампа́нского.

рестора́н

меню́		официа́нт
пе́рвое	второ́е	тре́тье
	напи́тки	

Прия́тного аппети́та!

мужска́я оде́жда

руба́шка	брю́ки
костю́м	га́лстук
трусы́	носки́
ма́йка	

же́нская оде́жда

блу́зка	ю́бка
пла́тье	шаль
бюстга́льтер	комбина́ция
тру́сики	колго́тки

магази́ны

Гастроно́м	Бу́лочная
О́вощи	Фру́кты
Конди́терская	Моро́женое

ры́нок

Ско́лько ве́сит?
Ско́лько сто́ит?

Я возьму́ сто грамм.
Да́йте мне пол-кило́.

парфюме́рия

зубна́я щётка	зубна́я па́ста
расчёска	салфе́тки
мы́ло	шампу́нь

апте́ка

Мне ну́жно что́-нибудь от

ка́шля	запо́ра	поно́са

У вас есть

аспири́н	щёлочь	бинт

the barber shop

I want
        a haircut and a shave.

Scissors-cut or razor cut?

the beauty salon

What can I do for you?

Give me a shampoo
        and a cut and set.

laundry and dry cleaning

Can you wash my underwear?

Can you iron my shirts?

jewelry items

I would like to buy

a bracelet	earrings
a necklace	a ring

stationery section

I have to buy a

pencil		pen
writing pad		writing paper
paperclips	and a	notebook

the newsstand

Do you have
        newspapers or magazines
        in English?

music

Which music do you like?
Classical or folk music?

Do you have
        an mp3-player or CD player?

souvenirs

nested doll	lacquer box
balalaika	fur hat

at the watchmaker

The watch is fast.
It is slow.
It doesn't run.
Can you replace the battery?

стирка и чистка

Вы мо́жете постира́ть моё бельё?

Вы мо́жете погла́дить э́ти руба́шки?

парикма́херская
же́нский зал

Что вам сде́лать?

Вы́мойте мне го́лову,
сде́лайте стри́жку и укла́дку.

парикма́херская
мужско́й зал

Я хочу́
постри́чься и побри́ться.

Но́жницами или бри́твой?

газе́тный кио́ск

У вас есть
газе́ты или жу́рналы
на англи́йском языке́?

канцеля́рский отде́л

Мне на́до купи́ть
каранда́ш   ру́чку
блокно́т   бума́гу для пи́сем
скре́пки   и   тетра́дь

ювели́рные изде́лия

Я хоте́л бы купи́ть
брасле́т   се́рьги
ожере́лье   кольцо́

ремо́нт часо́в

Они спеша́т.
Они отстаю́т.
Они стоя́т.
Мо́жно поста́вить но́вую батере́йку?

сувени́ры

матрешка   шкату́лка
балала́йка   ме́ховая ша́пка

музыка

Каку́ю му́зыку вы лю́бите?
Класси́ческую или наро́дную?

У вас есть
mp3-плеер или CD-плеер?

shoe repairs

heels   soles

shoelaces   insoles

repair of eyeglasses

Can you repair

    the lens
    the frame
    the earpiece

photography supplies

Do you develop film?
Twenty or thirty-six exposures?
Black and white or color?
Prints or slides?

the post office

I want to send to the USA
an airmail letter
a postcard
a fax

the bank

May I exchange money?
What is the exchange rate?

hard currency   travelers' checks
                cash

money

one kopeck   one ruble
two kopecks   two rubles
three kopecks   three rubles
four kopecks   four rubles
five kopecks   five rubles

What else hurts?

eyes   ears
heart   shoulder

I have a high temperature.
I don't feel well.

at the doctor

Doctor, my _____ hurts.

head   throat
arm   stomach
back   leg

telephones

I want to make
  an international call.

What is your telephone number?
Hello. This is Alexandra speaking.
I can't hear you. Speak louder.

фототовары

Вы проявля́ете плёнку?
Два́дцать или три́дцать шесть ка́дров?
Черно-бе́лые или цветны́е?
Фотока́рточки или сла́йды?

ремо́нт очко́в

Вы мо́жете почини́ть

стекло́
опра́ву
зау́шник

ремо́нт о́буви

каблуки́   подмётки

шнурки́   и сте́льки

Де́ньги

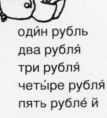

одна́ копе́йка
две копе́йки
три копе́йки
четы́ре копе́йки
пять копе́ек

оди́н рубль
два рубля́
три рубля́
четы́ре рубля́
пять рубле́й

банк

Мо́жно обменя́ть?
Како́й курс?

валю́та   доро́жные че́ки
    нали́чные

по́чта

Я хочу́ отпра́вить в США
авиаписьмо́
откры́тку
телефа́кс

телефо́н-автома́т

Я хочу́ заказа́ть
    междунаро́дный разгово́р.
      Како́й у вас но́мер телефо́на?
      Алло́, это говори́т
      Алекса́ндра.
      Пло́хо слы́шно. Говори́те
      гро́мче.

у врача́

До́ктор, у меня́ боли́т _____ .

голова́   го́рло
рука́   желу́док
спина́   нога́

Что ещё боли́т?

глаза́   у́ши
се́рдце   плечо́

У меня́ высо́кая температу́ра.
Я чу́вствую себя́ пло́хо.

Help!

Call

a doctor.
an ambulance.
the police.

the hospital

patient   nurse
operation   injection
pulse   blood pressure
medicine

at the dentist

I have a toothache.
I can put in a filling or
    pull the tooth!

colors

white   black
yellow   green
dark blue   light blue
red

Where is _____ ?

the restroom
the post office
the subway stop
the bus stop

Young man! (Waiter)

Miss! (Waitress)

important numbers

Fire   01
Police   02
Ambulance   03
US 911/European   112

My telephone number _____

Yes.
No.
That's great!
Why?
Because

I'm hungry.

I'm thirsty.
    (I want to drink something.)

зубно́й врач

У меня́ боли́т зуб.
Я могу́ поста́вить пло́мбу или
   удали́ть зуб!

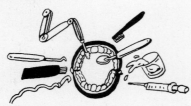

больни́ца

больно́й
опера́ция
пульс
лека́рство

медсестра́
уко́л
давле́ние кро́ви

Помоги́те!

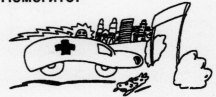

Вы́зовите

врача́.
ско́рую по́мощь.
мили́цию.

Молодо́й челове́к!

Де́вушка!

Где _____ ?

туале́т
по́чта
ста́нция метро́
остано́вка авто́буса

цвета́

бе́лый
жёлтый
си́ний
кра́сный

чёрный
зелёный
голубо́й

Я го́лоден.

Мне хо́чется пить.

Да.
Нет.
Хорошо́!
Пло́хо!
Почему́?
Потому́ что

Ва́жные номера́

Пожа́рная охра́на 01
Мили́ция 02
Ско́рая по́мощь 03
Еди́ный номер 112

Мой но́мер _____

to live
(1st conjugation verb)

I live	we live
you live	you live
he/she lives	they live

to run, jog
(1st conjugation verb)

I run	we run
you run	you run
she/he runs	they run

to speak, say
(2nd conjugation verb)

I speak	we speak
you speak	you speak
she/he speaks	they speak

the past tense

I, you, he (masculines)
    was, ran
I, you, she (feminines)
    was, ran
we, you, they (plurals)
    were, ran

(simple) future tense
with perfective verbs

I'll take	we'll take
you'll take	you'll take
he'll, she'll take	they'll take

future tense
with imperfective verbs

I will	we will
you will	you will
she will	they will
	speak.

yesterday

today

tomorrow

From where?

I am coming from the park.
We are coming from Moscow.
They are coming from a concert.
Are you coming from Vadim's?

Where to?

I am going to the park.
We are going to Moscow.
They are going to a concert.
Are you going to Vadim's?

говори́ть

я говорю́ — мы говори́м
ты говори́шь — вы говори́те
она/он говори́т — они говоря́т

бе́гать

я бе́гаю — мы бе́гаем
ты бе́гаешь — вы бе́гаете
она/он бе́гает — они бе́гают

жить

я живу́ — мы живём
ты живёшь — вы живёте
он/она живёт — они живу́т

бу́дущее вре́мя

я бу́ду — мы бу́дем
ты бу́дешь — вы бу́дете
она бу́дет — они бу́дут
говори́ть.

бу́дущее вре́мя

я возьму́ — мы возьмём
ты возьмёшь — вы возьмёте
он/она возьмёт — они возьму́т

проше́дшее вре́мя

я, ты, он
был, бе́гал
я, ты, она
была́, бе́гала
мы, вы, они
бы́ли, бе́гали

Куда́?

Я иду́ в парк.
Мы е́дем в Москву́.
Они иду́т на конце́рт.
Вы идёте к Ва́диму?

Отку́да?

Я иду́ из па́рка.
Мы е́дем из Москвы́.
Они иду́т с конце́рта.
Вы идёте от Ва́дима?

вчера́

сего́дня

за́втра

The Spelling Rules

1. After eight letters you may not write **я** or **ю**.

2. After seven letters you may not write **ы**.

3. After five letters you may not write **o** unless it is stressed.

Pronunciation Tips

1. When the letter **o** is not under stress it is pronounced as an **a**.

2. There are five "hard" vowels and five "soft" vowels.

3. At the end of a word, some consonants lose voicing; a **б** sounds like **п**.

A

B

C

Russian style!

neuter noun ending in o

window	Nominative case
Who is at the window?	Genitive
He approached the window.	Dative
They're looking out the window.	Accusative
This is next to the window.	Instrumental
The book is on the window.	Prepositional

feminine noun ending in a

Nina	Nominative case
Nina has time.	Genitive
They gave to Nina.	Dative
Who has seen Nina?	Accusative
What's with Nina?	Instrumental
What did you say about Nina?	Prepositional

masculine noun (hard)

Ivan	Nominative case
Ivan has money.	Genitive
They telephoned Ivan.	Dative
I know Ivan.	Accusative
We spoke with Ivan.	Instrumental
Mama is thinking about Ivan.	Prepositional

neuter noun ending in e

sea	Nominative case
Who was at the sea?	Genitive
He approached the sea.	Dative
They're looking into the sea.	Accusative
This is next to the sea.	Instrumental
The ship is on the sea.	Prepositional

feminine noun ending in я

Katya	Nominative case
Katya has time.	Genitive
They gave (it) to Katya.	Dative
Who has seen Katya?	Accusative
What's with Katya?	Instrumental
What did you say about Katya?	Prepositional

masculine noun (soft)

the driver	Nominative case
The driver has money.	Genitive
They telephoned the driver.	Dative
I know the driver.	Accusative
We spoke with the driver.	Instrumental
Mama's thinking about the driver.	Prepositional

азбука

а, 6, в, г, д, е, ё, ж, з, и, й,

к, л, м, н, о, п, р, с, т, у, ф,

х, ц, ч, ш, щ, ъ, ы, ь, э, ю, я

---

1. ´о → а

2. а, э, ы, о, у

    я, е, и, ё, ю

3. б → п, г → к, д → т
    ж → ш, з → с

---

1. ж, ш, щ, ч, ц, к, г, х
   я → а ю → у

2. ж, ш, щ, ч, к, г, х
   ы → и

3. ж, ш, щ, ч, ц
   ´о → е

Ива́н

У Ива́на есть де́ньги.
Позвони́ли Ива́ну.
Я зна́ю Ива́на.
Мы говори́ли с Ива́ном.
Ма́ма ду́мает об Ива́не.

Нина

У Ни́ны есть вре́мя.
Да́ли Ни́не.
Кто ви́дел Ни́ну?
Что с Ни́ной?
Что вы сказа́ли о Ни́не?

окно́

Кто стои́т у окна́.
Он подошёл к окну́.
Они́ смо́трят в окно́.
Это ря́дом с окно́м.
Кни́га на окне́.

води́тель

У води́теля есть де́ньгиг.
Позвони́ли води́телю.
Я зна́ю води́теля.
Мы говори́ли с води́телем.
Мама ду́мает о води́теле.

Ка́тя

У Ка́ти есть вре́мя.
Да́ли Ка́те.
Кто ви́дел Ка́тю?
Что с Ка́тей?
Что вы сказа́ли о Ка́те?

мо́ре

Кто был у мо́ря?
Он подошёл к мо́рю.
Они́ смо́трят в мо́ре.
Это ря́дом с мо́рем.
Ло́дка на мо́ре.

Computers

copy	cut	laptop	Open	Close
		printer		
paste	delete	scanner	Save	Print
		mp3-player		

Internet

news	pictures	Search	Click	Connect
		Find		
video	goods	Log off	Download	Enter
		Log in name		
		Password		

Search engines

file	folder	Google	On line Cyrillic keyboard
font	icon	Rambler	
keyboard	mouse	Yandex	Dictionaries
memory	monitor		

компьютеры

открыть   закры́ть

сохранить   напеча́тать

но́утбук
при́нтер
ска́нер
mp3-пле́ер

скопи́ровать   вы́резать

вста́вить   удали́ть

интернет

щёлкнуть   подключи́ться

загрузить   ввести́

поиска́ть
найти́
вы́йти
логи́н
паро́ль

но́вости   карти́нки

ви́део   това́ры

ПОИСКОВИКИ

он-ла́йн клавиату́ра
www.yandex.ru/index_engl_qwerty.html
словари́
www.freedict.com/onldict/rus.html

Google   google.ru
Rambler   rambler.ru
Yahoo   ru.yahoo.com
Yandex   yandex.ru

фа́йл   па́пка
шри́фт   ико́на
клавиату́ра   мышь
па́мять   монито́р